Low-Fodmap Air Fryer Cookbook

365-Day Delicious Gluten-Free, Allergy-Friendly Air Fryer Recipes to Relieve the Symptoms of IBS and Other Digestive Disorders

Megon Buckey

Table of Contents

Chapter 6: Beef Pork & Lamb Recipes 76

Chapter 7: Seafood & Fish Recipes 96

Chapter 8: Meatless Meals Recipes 116

Introduction

Simple Gluten-Free, low-Fodmap recipes anyone can make, without too many expensive equipment or complicated steps, just need an air fryer. It can heal your digestive problems, heal your stomach, balance your spirit, and result in a healthier, happier you. This recipe will ignite your passion for cooking and baking, and will be suitable for everyone who is sensitive to the stomach.

This cookbook includes all the low fodmap foods in every recipe, as well as plenty of easy to read shopping guides. It will provide you with a perfect meal plan and put you on the right track. Every ingredient is easily found in the supermarket.

This Low-Fodmap Air Fryer cookbook provides nutritionally sound advice with delicious and approachable recipes to help those with IBS not only feel better-but to thrive.

Chapter 1: Low-Fodmap Diet Basic

Key to a Healthy Gut

Our Gastrointestinal Gut (GI), bowel, or gut has a pivotal role to play in preserving the health and life of our systems. This is the first organic body system that notes rapid growth during the first 3 years of our lives and continues to develop for the rest of our lives. Its primary role is to digest and break down the food we consume and facilitate nutrient absorption or waste/elimination of unwanted substances whenever necessary. Gut was also surprisingly found to have connections with the brain (the gut-brain axis) and the immune system, indirectly affecting their health.

The human gut reportedly hosts over 100 trillion microorganisms, generally known as 'microbiota' or 'microflora'. These include both beneficial and health-preserving bacteria (probiotics) as well as bad bacteria and parasites that may lead to various health symptoms if their population spans out of control.

Essentially, there are two schools of thought when it comes to improving gut health. The first is to increase or feed the population of beneficial bacteria that resides on the gut and the second is the reduction of bad bacteria or elimination of triggering substances from foods that may aggravate gut health. In many cases, these two approaches are used in tandem for deeper and more long-lasting results. This is essentially the key to optimal gut health in the long run.

The low FODMAP diet works by eliminating certain food triggers and depriving the bacterial population of feeding nutrients that they need to survive. However, since the diet might starve bad as well as good bacteria during the elimination phase, it is always a good idea to supplement your diet with probiotics so you don't lose any beneficial bacteria along the process.

Low Fodmap Diet as a Lifestyle

As specified earlier, the low FODMAP diet is not another diet fab for losing weight and getting shredded. It's a lifestyle choice that will improve gut health temporarily or for longer periods, as long as it is followed wisely and in moderation. Since over 50 million Americans suffer from digestive problems on a chronic basis and the global prevalence according to multinational studies reaches 40% of the adult population, it would be wise to follow a diet and lifestyle that improves chronic gut health.

IBS especially is a common disturbance that affects over 25 million Americans and approx. 15% of the total population worldwide. Common symptoms include bloating, gas, and abdominal pain. The symptoms can range from mild to severe and in some cases, they are so extreme that they cause disability and failure to keep up with daily life tasks e.g. work. Hence, a diet that manages these symptoms e.g. the low FODMAP diet, is a diet that will give the sufferers their normal life back.

Many mistakenly think that the low FODMAP diet is only about the elimination of high FODMAP foods to control IBS symptoms but this isn't the case. The diet is only a part of a more holistic approach to achieving gut health. Paired with a healthy lifestyle e.g. no smoking, decreased stress, the effects of the diet will be more profound and lasting.

What Causes IBS and Digestive Disorders

Patients and doctors have noticed for quite a long time that certain foods and substances may trigger IBS and similar digestive symptoms e.g., gas, bloating irregular bowel movements. Some well-known food triggers, as mentioned earlier are lactose, fructose, alcohol, etc. These are often found in certain dairy products, legumes, nuts, grains, cruciferous veggies, and fruits. Some of these have been found to cause gas and should be avoided in cases of vivid bloating and indigestion. However, up until a few decades ago, these certain foods appeared in the lists of foods to avoid for IBS without exactly identifying the common chemical attributes that these food triggers shared. Eventually, with the progress of science and technology that took off the last 40 years, these chemical substances were identified and classified as potential triggers for people who experience IBS and other digestive problems. The poor digestion and malabsorption of these short chain carbs have been described by medical researchers as the culprit of gas, bloating, diarrhea, nausea, and abdominal pain in patients diagnosed with IBS. The earliest reports have identified 5 particular culprits, categorized based on their chemical form:

- Lactose. Early studies that date back to the 50s and 60s have found a link between lactose and diarrhea symptoms. Ever since there have been numerous lab diagnostic means to check lactose responses and diagnose intolerance. In intolerant patients with digestive issues, doctors have advised the elimination of lactose from the patient's diet, however, this has been found to ease only some symptoms of IBS and not solve the matter completely.
- Fructose & Sorbitol. Fructose is a type of monosaccharide sugar that is naturally found in fruits. Sorbitol is also similar to sugar alcohol and carb found in certain fruits like figs and plums. Although not many studies have found a clear link between fructose/sorbitol and IBS symptoms, a few studies have found that fructose or low fructose and sorbitol diet has eased IBS symptoms in patients that

didn't respond to other methods of treatment or lactose elimination.

- Oligosaccharides. Oligosaccharides (oligos or oligo-fructans) stand for the "O" in "FODMAP" and refer to sugar alcohols that contain up to 10 linked monosaccharide units~in simple words, they are classified as "simple sugars". These include both natural and artificial sweeteners. Beans and some veggies e.g. Jerusalem artichokes are also high in oligos. Our systems though have been found to lack the enzymes necessary to digest and fully absorb oligos, resulting in flatulence (gas) and constipation.
- Polyols. Polyols (standing for the "P" in FODMAP) are sugar alcohols that occur naturally in certain fruits and artificial sweeteners like mannitol and xylitol. Their ability to aggravate gut symptoms was first discovered in a 60s study and there have been studies ever since backing up the link between polyps and induced gut symptoms, especially when combined with fructose and sorbitol. However, in moderate doses polyps have been found to have a beneficial effect on the gut's biome, increasing the numbers of beneficial bacteria in the gut.

The common pattern here is that these substances lead collectively to indigestion (lactose), malabsorption (fructose, sorbitol, polyols), and fermentation (oligos) which ultimately lead to IBS and digestive disorders when they are consumed in high amounts.

Stress and other lifestyle factors may also be clear culprits of IBS symptoms; however, a few studies have found that they may worsen already existing symptoms in IBS-affected patients. Therefore, a low FODMAP diet followed periodically coupled with a healthy lifestyle may be the answer for the effective reduction of IBS symptoms.

Low Fodmap Diet Targets & Benefits

By now, you already realize that the main purpose of a low FODMAP diet is to treat IBS and other digestive problems. A short-term or occasionally followed low FODMAP diet has been found to effectively treat the symptoms that come with the fermentation, indigestion, or malabsorption of certain carbs and substances in those who are intolerant to these. More specifically, a low FODMAP diet can result in:

- Less gas/flatulence. Due to the decreased fermentation of sugar carbs in the digestive tract, the system will be able to release less gas. In one particular UK study, it has been found that 87% of the study participants who followed a low FODMAP diet have noted a significant decrease in gas production/flatulence as opposed to 49% of the control group.
- Less bloating. In the same study above, the study's subjects who followed a low

FODMAP diet have shown an impressive decrease of their bloating symptoms by as much as 82% compared to 49% of those that did not follow the low FODMAP diet.

- Less abdominal pain. In a study involving big children aged 7-18, it has been found that the children who followed a low FODMAP diet had less intense abdominal pain episodes compared to the children participants who followed another diet type (TACD).
- Less diarrhea. A US study conducted in 110 adult patients with diarrhea-predominant IBS symptoms, has shown that the patients' group who followed a low FODMAP diet had fewer diarrhea episodes and noted better stool frequency than those who followed a GDA (Guideline Daily Amounts) diet.

Although symptoms and their severity may vary between IBS patients, there is plenty of evidence pointing out significant improvements in bloating, gas, abdominal pain, and diarrhea in patients who follow the diet for a few weeks. Therefore, if you experience any of the above, your symptoms will most likely improve, if you follow the low FODMAP diet properly.

List of Ingredients to Avoid

The actual foods and ingredients that are high on FODMAPS and may, in turn, aggravate IBS symptoms are the following (we have broken this down to 5 main categories and subcategories so you can check easily which foods to avoid when you are in the first stage of the low FODMAP diet).

Fruits:

- Apples
- Apricots
- Blackberries
- Cherries
- Mangoes
- Nectarines
- Pears
- Plums
- Prunes
- Watermelon
- Dried fruits e.g. apricots, figs, etc.

Vegetables:

- Artichokes
- Asparagus
- Beetroot
- Broccoli
- Brussel sprouts
- Cauliflower
- Celery
- Garlic

- Leeks
- Mushrooms

- Onions
- Sweet Corn

Legumes:

- Beans (all kinds)

- Lentils

Nuts:

- Cashew Nuts

- Pistachios

Sugars:

- Agave nectar
- Corn Syrup
- Fructose
- Honey

- Maltitol
- Sorbitol
- Xylitol

Wheat products (with gluten):

- Cereals
- Crackers
- Bread

- Pasta
- Pizza

Dairy:

- Cow milk
- Custard
- Ice cream

- Pudding
- Soft cheeses e.g. cottage cheese
- Yogurt

Drinks:

- Alcohol

- Sports & energy drinks with artificial sweeteners

Best Tips to Succeed In the Kitchen With Low Fodmap Diet

Following a low FODMAP diet can be a tad challenging for newbies
however, don't let the list of "foods to avoid" fool you and limit your cooking options. There are just as many if not more cooking ingredients to explore and you can prepare low FODMAP meals much easier if you follow these kitchen tips. Here they are:

Tip #1: Prepare your meals in advance.

If you don't have the time and energy to prepare your low FODMAP meal for the day, choose 1-2 days a week based on your schedule to prepare a week's worth of low FODMAP meals in advance. Make a shopping list of what you'll need (in case you don't have the necessary recipe ingredients already), go shopping, and spare 2-3 hours every time to prepare your weekly meals. You can also keep any leftovers in the freezer if you plan to prepare larger batches of food.

Tip#2: Make your condiments and dressings.

Most store-bought condiments and dressings e.g ketchup contain hidden amounts of processed or natural sugars which are the worst triggering FODMAPs for IBS patients. If you are not sure whether a condiment or dressing is low FODMAP, check its label and avoid anything that contains corn syrup, maltitol, fructose, or any other sugar from the prohibited list. If the recipe calls it, prepare your own using natural ingredients and low FODMAP sweetener alternatives such as maple syrup or Stevia.

Tip# 3: Go for lactose-free dairy options.

There is no need to quit eating dairy altogether when you are on a low FODMAP diet as there are some dairy options that contain low to zero amounts of lactose and thus are low on FODMAPs. Some good low or lactose-free options include dry/mature cheeses, lactose-free milk, and lactose-free yogurt. Vegetarian dairy alternatives like almond milk and soy yogurt are perfectly fine as long as they don't contain any FODMAP sugar types.

Tip#4: Use spices in place of onions and garlic.

Avoiding onions and garlic is a bit challenging as most recipes nowadays use these to add some flavor and dimension to the dish, however, you can counteract their lack by using flavorful spices e.g. curry, coriander, cumin, chili flakes. Nearly all spices (apart from garlic and onion powder obviously) are perfectly fine to use in a low FODMAP diet and there is no limit to their amounts- -it's a matter of how hot or spicy you like your food.

Tip#5: Saute your meat and veggies first.

In addition to using spices in your dishes in place of onion and garlic, you can add more flavor to your dishes by browning your meat and veggies first in a bit of vegetable oil. You can also make your onion and garlic-free stock by browning low FODMAP veggies e.g carrots and parsnips and adding at least 4 cups of boiling water, salt, herbs, and spices. Once your stock is ready, you can keep it in the fridge for up to 1 week (to use later on your weekly meals) or in the freezer for up to 2 months, in the form of ice-cubes so you can use 1-2 cubes every time you need it for the recipe.

Positive Vibes from the Author

Following a low FODMAP diet isn't as challenging as some people assume. If you prepare your meals in advance, check your portions, and experiment with low FODMAP alternatives for at least a week, things will be much easier afterward. Keep in mind that during the final stages, you may re-introduce some foods that are higher in FODMAPs to see your gut's reaction, and based on our research, most people are affected by one type of FODMAP more than others. So don't worry, you won't have to quit eating all the foods on the prohibited list for long periods and restrict yourself. And if you are stuck or don't know what else you should cook, check out our recipes or join an online FODMAP diet community to draw some inspiration and support from people like you who are already following the diet. Even better, you may seek the professional advice and support of a nutritionist who has experience in treating patients with digestive disorders, especially IBS. Don't be afraid to ask for help sometimes it's best to have someone on your side instead of going through your diet journey alone.

Remember: Low FODMAP is not just another diet fad, it's a lifestyle choice and your gut will thank you for it!

Chapter 2: Air Fryer Basics

What is an Air Fryer?

An air fryer is one of the magical cooking appliances which help to cook various delicious and tasty dishes at home. The air fryer works like a convection oven. It cooks food by circulating very hot air into an air fryer chamber. You can fry French fries with very less oil required. It saves more than 80percent of oil while frying or cooking food. Most of the people are disappointed due to the lack of crispiness in their food. The air fryer makes your food crispy and tasty.

Air fryer circulates hot air into food basket with the help of a fan. These fans are located on the top of the food basket. Using this fan air fryer circulates quick and even air around the food basket. Due to this, your food is cook evenly on all sides. It is one of the best choices for those people who love fried food most but also hate about the extra calories.

The Benefits of Air Fryer

The air fryer comes with various benefits some of them are described as follows:

1. **Requires less oil and fats**

Compare to other traditional fryer Air fryer requires very less oil to fry. It saves more than 80 percent of oil during cooking. Just a tablespoon of oil fries your French fries make it tender from inside and crispy from outside.

2. **Saves nutritional values**

Traditional deep-frying method destroys essential vitamin and minerals from your food. Air fryer fries your food by blowing the very hot air into a food basket. Air frying your food helps to maintain essential vitamins and nutrients into your food.

3. **Versatile cooking options**

Air fryer is not only used for frying purpose but also cooks, roasts, grill and bake delicious food for you. It works like a multi-cooker do all the operations into a single pot.

4. **Reduce the risk of heart-related disease**

Eating deep-fried food is not a healthy choice for your body. Air fryer requires very less oil to fry your food. It also maintains essential vitamins and nutrients into your food. This will help to reduce heart-related disease.

5. Automatic cooking programs

Most of the air fryer comes with pre-programmed auto cook buttons. These auto cooking functions are nothing but commonly used programs like French fries, chicken fries, chips, etc. You just need to press auto cook function button your air fryer automatically adjusts the time and temperature of your air fryer.

Chapter 3: Snack & Appetizers Recipes

Perfect Crab Dip

Preparation Time: 5 minutes
Cooking Time: 7 minutes
Serve:4
Ingredients:

- 1 cup crabmeat
- 2 tbsp parsley, chopped
- 2 tbsp fresh lemon juice
- 2 tbsp hot sauce
- 1/2 cup green onion, sliced
- 2 cups cheese, grated
- 1/4 cup mayonnaise
- 1/4 tsp pepper
- 1/2 tsp salt

Directions:

1. In a 6-inch dish, mix together crabmeat, hot sauce, cheese, mayo, pepper, and salt.
2. Place dish in air fryer basket and cook dip at 400 F for 7 minutes.
3. Remove dish from air fryer.
4. Drizzle dip with lemon juice and garnish with parsley.
5. Serve and enjoy.

Nutritional Value (Amount per Serving):

- Calories 313
- Fat 23.9 g
- Carbohydrates 8.8 g
- Sugar 3.1 g
- Protein 16.2 g
- Cholesterol 67 mg

Spinach Dip

Preparation Time: 10 minutes
Cooking Time: 40 minutes
Serve:8

Ingredients:

- 8 oz cream cheese, softened
- 1/4 tsp garlic powder
- 1/2 cup onion, minced
- 1/3 cup water chestnuts, drained and chopped
- 1 cup mayonnaise
- 1 cup parmesan cheese, grated
- 1 cup frozen spinach, thawed and squeeze out all liquid
- 1/2 tsp pepper

Directions:

1. Spray air fryer baking dish with cooking spray.
2. Add all ingredients into the bowl and mix until well combined.
3. Transfer bowl mixture into the prepared baking dish and place dish in air fryer basket.
4. Cook at 300 F for 35-40 minutes. After 20 minutes of cooking stir dip.
5. Serve and enjoy.

Nutritional Value (Amount per Serving):

- Calories 220
- Fat 20.5 g
- Carbohydrates 9.3 g
- Sugar 2.3 g
- Protein 3.8 g
- Cholesterol 41 mg

Shrimp Kabobs

Preparation Time: 10 minutes
Cooking Time: 8 minutes
Serve: 2

Ingredients:

- 1 cup shrimp
- 1 lime juice
- 1 garlic clove, minced
- 1/4 tsp pepper
- 1/8 tsp salt

Directions:

1. Preheat the air fryer to 350 F.
2. Add shrimp, lime juice, garlic, pepper, and salt into the bowl and toss well.
3. Thread shrimp onto the soaked wooden skewers and place into the air fryer basket.
4. Cook for 8 minutes. Turn halfway through.
5. Serve and enjoy.

Nutritional Value (Amount per Serving):

- Calories 75
- Fat 1 g
- Carbohydrates 4 g
- Sugar 0.5 g
- Protein 13 g
- Cholesterol 160 mg

Easy Jalapeno Poppers

Preparation Time: 10 minutes
Cooking Time: 13 minutes
Serve:5

Ingredients:

- 5 jalapeno peppers, slice in half and deseeded
- 2 tbsp salsa
- 4 oz goat cheese, crumbled
- 1/4 tsp chili powder
- 1/2 tsp garlic, minced
- Pepper
- Salt

Directions:

1. In a small bowl, mix together cheese, salsa, chili powder, garlic, pepper, and salt.
2. Spoon cheese mixture into each jalapeno halves and place in air fryer basket.
3. Cook jalapeno poppers at 350 F for 13 minutes.
4. Serve and enjoy.

Nutritional Value (Amount per Serving):

- Calories 111
- Fat 8.3 g
- Carbohydrates 2.1 g
- Sugar 1.2 g
- Protein 7.3 g
- Cholesterol 24 mg

Veggie Cream Stuff Mushrooms

Preparation Time: 10 minutes
Cooking Time: 8 minutes
Serve: 12

Ingredients:

- 24 oz mushrooms, cut stems
- 1/2 cup sour cream
- 1 cup cheddar cheese, shredded
- 1 small carrot, diced
- 1/2 bell pepper, diced
- 1/2 onion, diced
- 2 bacon slices, diced

Directions:

1. Chop mushroom stems finely.
2. Spray pan with cooking spray and heat over medium heat.
3. Add chopped mushrooms, bacon, carrot, onion, and bell pepper into the pan and cook until tender.
4. Remove pan from heat. Add cheese and sour cream into the cooked vegetables and stir well.
5. Stuff vegetable mixture into the mushroom cap and place into the air fryer basket.
6. Cook mushrooms at 350 F for 8 minutes.
7. Serve and enjoy.

Nutritional Value (Amount per Serving):

- Calories 93
- Fat 6.6 g
- Carbohydrates 3.7 g
- Sugar 1.7 g
- Protein 5.7 g
- Cholesterol 18 mg

Air Fried Cheese Sticks

Preparation Time: 10 minutes
Cooking Time: 8 minutes
Serve: 4 minutes

Ingredients:

- 6 mozzarella cheese sticks
- 1/4 tsp garlic powder
- 1 tsp Italian seasoning
- 1/3 cup almond flour
- 1/2 cup parmesan cheese, grated
- 1 large egg, lightly beaten
- 1/4 tsp sea salt

Directions:

1. In a small bowl, whisk the egg.
2. In a shallow bowl, mix together almond flour, parmesan cheese, Italian seasoning, garlic powder, and salt.
3. Dip mozzarella cheese stick in egg then coat with almond flour mixture and place on a plate. Place in refrigerator for 1 hour.
4. Spray air fryer basket with cooking spray.
5. Place prepared mozzarella cheese sticks into the air fryer basket and cook at 375 F for 8 minutes.
6. Serve and enjoy.

Nutritional Value (Amount per Serving):

- Calories 245
- Fat 18 g
- Carbohydrates 3 g
- Sugar 2 g
- Protein 19 g
- Cholesterol 0 mg

Yummy Chicken Dip

Preparation Time: 10 minutes
Cooking Time: 20 minutes
Serve: 6

Ingredients:

- 2 cups chicken, cooked and shredded
- 3/4 cup sour cream
- 1/4 tsp onion powder
- 8 oz cream cheese, softened
- 3 tbsp hot sauce
- 1/4 tsp garlic powder

Directions:

1. Preheat the air fryer to 325 F.
2. Add all ingredients in a large bowl and mix until well combined.
3. Transfer mixture in air fryer baking dish and place in the air fryer.
4. Cook chicken dip for 20 minutes.
5. Serve and enjoy.

Nutritional Value (Amount per Serving):

- Calories 245
- Fat 17 g
- Carbohydrates 1.5 g
- Sugar 0.2 g
- Protein 16 g
- Cholesterol 85 mg

Crab Mushrooms

Preparation Time: 10 minutes
Cooking Time: 8 minutes
Serve: 16

Ingredients:

- 16 mushrooms, clean and chop stems
- 1/4 tsp chili powder
- 1/4 tsp onion powder
- 1/4 cup mozzarella cheese, shredded
- 2 oz crab meat, chopped
- 8 oz cream cheese, softened
- 2 tsp garlic, minced
- 1/4 tsp pepper

Directions:

1. In a mixing bowl, mix together stems, chili powder, onion powder, pepper, cheese, crabmeat, cream cheese, and garlic until well combined.
2. Stuff mushrooms with bowl mixture and place into the air fryer basket.
3. Cook mushrooms at 370 F for 8 minutes.
4. Serve and enjoy.

Nutritional Value (Amount per Serving):

- Calories 59
- Fat 5.1 g
- Carbohydrates 1.2 g
- Sugar 0.4 g
- Protein 2.2 g
- Cholesterol 18 mg

Easy Carrot Dip

Preparation Time: 10 minutes
Cooking Time: 15 minutes
Serve: 6

Ingredients:

- 2 cups carrots, grated
- 1/4 tsp cayenne pepper
- 4 tbsp butter, melted
- 1 tbsp chives, chopped
- Pepper
- Salt

Directions:

1. Add all ingredients into the air fryer baking dish and stir until well combined.
2. Place dish in the air fryer and cook at 380 F for 15 minutes.
3. Transfer cook carrot mixture into the blender and blend until smooth.
4. Serve and enjoy.

Nutritional Value (Amount per Serving):

- Calories 83
- Fat 7.7 g
- Carbohydrates 3.7 g
- Sugar 1.8 g
- Protein 0.4 g
- Cholesterol 20 mg

Sweet Potato Tots

Preparation Time: 10 minutes
Cooking Time: 31 minutes
Serve: 24

Ingredients:

- 2 sweet potatoes, peeled
- 1/2 tsp cajun seasoning
- Salt

Directions:

1. Add water in large pot and bring to boil. Add sweet potatoes in pot and boil for 15 minutes. Drain well.
2. Grated boil sweet potatoes into a large bowl using a grated.
3. Add cajun seasoning and salt in grated sweet potatoes and mix until well combined.
4. Spray air fryer basket with cooking spray.
5. Make small tot of sweet potato mixture and place in air fryer basket.
6. Cook at 400 F for 8 minutes. Turn tots to another side and cook for 8 minutes more.
7. Serve and enjoy.

Nutritional Value (Amount per Serving):

- Calories 15
- Fat 0 g
- Carbohydrates 3.5 g
- Sugar 0.1 g
- Protein 0.2 g
- Cholesterol 0 mg

Parmesan Zucchini Bites

Preparation Time: 10 minutes
Cooking Time: 10 minutes
Serve: 6

Ingredients:

- 1 egg, lightly beaten
- 4 zucchinis, grated and squeeze out all liquid
- 1 cup shredded coconut
- 1 tsp Italian seasoning
- 1/2 cup parmesan cheese, grated

Directions:

1. Add all ingredients into the bowl and mix until well combined.
2. Spray air fryer basket with cooking spray.
3. Make small balls from zucchini mixture and place into the air fryer basket and cook at 400 F for 10 minutes.
4. Serve and enjoy.

Nutritional Value (Amount per Serving):

- Calories 88
- Fat 6.2 g
- Carbohydrates 6.6 g
- Sugar 3.2 g
- Protein 3.7 g
- Cholesterol 29 mg

Cabbage Chips

Preparation Time: 10 minutes
Cooking Time: 30 minutes
Serve: 6

Ingredients:

- 1 large cabbage head, tear cabbage leaves into pieces
- 2 tbsp olive oil
- 1/4 cup parmesan cheese, grated
- Pepper
- Salt

Directions:

1. Preheat the air fryer to 250 F.
2. Add all ingredients into the large mixing bowl and toss well.
3. Spray air fryer basket with cooking spray.
4. Divide cabbage in batches.
5. Add one cabbage chips batch in air fryer basket and cook for 25-30 minutes at 250 F or until chips are crispy and lightly golden brown.
6. Serve and enjoy.

Nutritional Value (Amount per Serving):

- Calories 96
- Fat 5.1 g
- Carbohydrates 12.1 g
- Sugar 6.7 g
- Protein 3 g
- Cholesterol 1 mg

Daikon Chips

Preparation Time: 10 minutes
Cooking Time: 16 minutes
Serve: 6

Ingredients:

- 15 oz Daikon, slice into chips
- 1 tbsp olive oil
- 1 tsp chili powder
- 1/2 tsp pepper
- 1 tsp salt

Directions:

1. Preheat the air fryer to 375 F.
2. Add all ingredients into the bowl and toss to coat.
3. Transfer sliced the daikon into the air fryer basket and cook for 16 minutes. Toss halfway through.
4. Serve and enjoy.

Nutritional Value (Amount per Serving):

- Calories 36
- Fat 2.4 g
- Carbohydrates 3.2 g
- Sugar 1.5 g
- Protein 1.5 g
- Cholesterol 0 mg

Rangoon Crab Dip

Preparation Time: 10 minutes
Cooking Time: 16 minutes
Serve: 8

Ingredients:

- 2 cups crab meat
- 1 cup mozzarella cheese, shredded
- 1/2 tsp garlic powder
- 1/4 cup pimentos, drained and diced
- 1/4 tsp stevia
- 1/2 lemon juice
- 2 tsp coconut amino
- 2 tsp mayonnaise
- 8 oz cream cheese, softened
- 1 tbsp green onion
- 1/4 tsp pepper
- Salt

Directions:

1. Preheat the air fryer to 325 F.
2. Add all ingredients except half mozzarella cheese into the large bowl and mix until well combined.
3. Transfer bowl mixture into the air fryer baking dish and sprinkle with remaining mozzarella cheese.
4. Place into the air fryer and cook for 16 minutes.
5. Serve and enjoy.

Nutritional Value (Amount per Serving):

- Calories 141
- Fat 11.5 g
- Carbohydrates 4.9 g
- Sugar 1.7 g
- Protein 4.9 g
- Cholesterol 38 mg

Buffalo Cauliflower Wings

Preparation Time: 10 minutes
Cooking Time: 14 minutes
Serve:4

Ingredients:

- 1 cauliflower head, cut into florets
- 1 tbsp butter, melted
- 1/2 cup buffalo sauce
- Pepper
- Salt

Directions:

1. Spray air fryer basket with cooking spray.
2. In a bowl, mix together buffalo sauce, butter, pepper, and salt.
3. Add cauliflower florets into the air fryer basket and cook at 400 F for 7 minutes.
4. Transfer cauliflower florets into the buffalo sauce mixture and toss well.
5. Again, add cauliflower florets into the air fryer basket and cook for 7 minutes more at 400 F.
6. Serve and enjoy.

Nutritional Value (Amount per Serving):

- Calories 44
- Fat 3 g
- Carbohydrates 3.8 g
- Sugar 1.6 g
- Protein 1.3 g
- Cholesterol 8 mg

Jalapeno Cheese Dip

Preparation Time: 10 minutes
Cooking Time: 16 minutes
Serve: 6

Ingredients:

- 1 1/2 cup Monterey jack cheese, shredded
- 1 1/2 cup cheddar cheese, shredded
- 2 jalapeno pepper, minced
- 1 tsp garlic powder
- 1/3 cup sour cream
- 1/3 cup mayonnaise
- 8 oz cream cheese, softened
- 8 bacon slices, cooked and crumbled
- Pepper
- Salt

Directions:

1. Preheat the air fryer to 325 F.
2. Add all ingredients into the bowl and mix until combined.
3. Transfer bowl mixture into the air fryer baking dish and place in the air fryer and cook for 16 minutes.
4. Serve and enjoy.

Nutritional Value (Amount per Serving):

- Calories 569
- Fat 48.7 g
- Carbohydrates 6.2 g
- Sugar 1.5 g
- Protein 26.8 g
- Cholesterol 133 mg

Flavorful Pork Meatballs

Preparation Time: 10 minutes
Cooking Time: 10 minutes
Serve: 4

Ingredients:

- 2 eggs, lightly beaten
- 2 tbsp capers
- 1/2 lb ground pork
- 3 garlic cloves, minced
- 2 tbsp fresh mint, chopped
- 1/2 tbsp cilantro, chopped
- 2 tsp red pepper flakes, crushed
- 1 1/2 tbsp butter, melted
- 1 tsp kosher salt

Directions:

1. Preheat the air fryer to 395 F.
2. Add all ingredients into the mixing bowl and mix until well combined.
3. Spray air fryer basket with cooking spray.
4. Make small balls from meat mixture and place into the air fryer basket.
5. Cook meatballs for 10 minutes. Shake basket halfway through.
6. Serve and enjoy.

Nutritional Value (Amount per Serving):

- Calories 159
- Fat 8.7 g
- Carbohydrates 1.9 g
- Sugar 0.3 g
- Protein 18.1 g
- Cholesterol 135 mg

Sesame Okra

Preparation Time: 10 minutes
Cooking Time: 4 minutes
Serve: 4

Ingredients:

- 11 oz okra, wash and chop
- 1 egg, lightly beaten
- 1 tsp sesame seeds
- 1 tbsp sesame oil
- 1/4 tsp pepper
- 1/2 tsp salt

Directions:

1. In a bowl, whisk together egg, pepper, and salt.
2. Add okra into the whisked egg. Sprinkle with sesame seeds.
3. Preheat the air fryer to 400 F.
4. Stir okra well. Spray air fryer basket with cooking spray.
5. Place okra pieces into the air fryer basket and cook for 4 minutes.
6. Serve and enjoy.

Nutritional Value (Amount per Serving):

- Calories 82
- Fat 5 g
- Carbohydrates 6.2 g
- Sugar 1.2 g
- Protein 3 g
- Cholesterol 41 mg

Healthy Toasted Nuts

Preparation Time: 10 minutes
Cooking Time: 9 minutes
Serve: 4

Ingredients:

- 1/2 cup macadamia nuts
- 1/2 cup pecans
- 1 tbsp olive oil
- 1/4 cup walnuts
- 1/4 cup hazelnuts
- 1 tsp salt

Directions:

1. Preheat the air fryer to 320 F.
2. Add all nuts into the air fryer basket and cook for 8 minutes. Shake halfway through.
3. Drizzle nuts with olive oil and season with salt and toss well.
4. Cook nuts for 1 minute more.
5. Serve and enjoy.

Nutritional Value (Amount per Serving):

- Calories 240
- Fat 24.9 g
- Carbohydrates 4.1 g
- Sugar 1.1 g
- Protein 4.1 g
- Cholesterol 0 mg

Air Fry Bacon

Preparation Time: 5 minutes
Cooking Time: 10 minutes
Serve:11
Ingredients:

- 11 bacon slices

Directions:

1. Place half bacon slices in air fryer basket.
2. Cook at 400 F for 10 minutes.
3. Cook remaining half bacon slices using same steps.
4. Serve and enjoy.

Nutritional Value (Amount per Serving):

- Calories 103
- Fat 7.9 g
- Carbohydrates 0.3 g
- Sugar 0 g
- Protein 7 g
- Cholesterol 21 mg

Chapter 4: Brunch Recipes

Radish Hash Browns

Preparation Time: 10 minutes

Cooking Time: 13 minutes

Serve: 4

Ingredients:

- 1 lb radishes, washed and cut off roots
- 1 tbsp olive oil
- 1/2 tsp paprika
- 1/2 tsp onion powder
- 1/2 tsp garlic powder
- 1 medium onion
- 1/4 tsp pepper
- 3/4 tsp sea salt

Directions:

1. Slice onion and radishes using a mandolin slicer.
2. Add sliced onion and radishes in a large mixing bowl and toss with olive oil.
3. Transfer onion and radish slices in air fryer basket and cook at 360 F for 8 minutes. Shake basket twice.
4. Return onion and radish slices in a mixing bowl and toss with seasonings.
5. Again, cook onion and radish slices in air fryer basket for 5 minutes at 400 F. Shake basket halfway through.
6. Serve and enjoy.

Nutritional Value (Amount per Serving):

- Calories 62
- Fat 3.7 g
- Carbohydrates 7.1 g
- Sugar 3.5 g
- Protein 1.2 g
- Cholesterol 0 mg

Breakfast Casserole

Preparation Time: 10 minutes
Cooking Time: 28 minutes
Serve: 4

Ingredients:

- 2 eggs
- 4 egg whites
- 4 tsp pine nuts, minced
- 2/3 cup chicken broth
- 1 lb Italian sausage
- 1/4 cup roasted red pepper, sliced
- 1/4 cup pesto sauce
- 2/3 cup parmesan cheese, grated
- 1/8 tsp pepper
- 1/4 tsp sea salt

Directions:

1. Preheat the air fryer to 370 F.
2. Spray air fryer pan with cooking spray and set aside.
3. Heat another pan over medium heat. Add sausage in a pan and cook until golden brown.
4. Once cooked then drain excess oil and spread it into the prepared pan.
5. Whisk remaining ingredients except pine nuts in a bowl and pour over sausage.
6. Place pan in the air fryer and cook for 25-28 minutes.
7. Top with pine nuts and serve.

Nutritional Value (Amount per Serving):

- Calories 625
- Fat 49 g
- Carbohydrates 2 g
- Sugar 2.1 g
- Protein 39 g
- Cholesterol 200 mg

Vegetable Egg Cups

Preparation Time:10 minutes
Cooking Time:20 minutes
Serve:4

Ingredients:

- 4 eggs
- 1 tbsp cilantro, chopped
- 4 tbsp half and half
- 1 cup cheddar cheese, shredded
- 1 cup vegetables, diced
- Pepper
- Salt

Directions:

1. Spray four ramekins with cooking spray and set aside.
2. In a mixing bowl, whisk eggs with cilantro, half and half, vegetables, 1/2 cup cheese, pepper, and salt.
3. Pour egg mixture into the four ramekins.
4. Place ramekins in air fryer basket and cook at 300 F for 12 minutes.
5. Top with remaining 1/2 cup cheese and cook for 2 minutes more at 400 F.
6. Serve and enjoy.

Nutritional Value (Amount per Serving):

- Calories 194
- Fat 11.5 g
- Carbohydrates 6 g
- Sugar 0.5 g
- Protein 13 g
- Cholesterol 190 mg

Egg Cups

Preparation Time: 10 minutes
Cooking Time: 18 minutes
Serve: 12

Ingredients:

- 12 eggs
- 4 oz cream cheese
- 12 bacon strips, uncooked
- 1/4 cup buffalo sauce
- 2/3 cup cheddar cheese, shredded
- Pepper
- Salt

Directions:

1. In a bowl, whisk together eggs, pepper, and salt.
2. Line each silicone muffin mold with one bacon strip.
3. Pour egg mixture into each muffin mold and place in the air fryer basket. (In batches)
4. Cook at 350 F for 8 minutes.
5. In another bowl, mix together cheddar cheese and cream cheese and microwave for 30 seconds. Add buffalo sauce and stir well.
6. Remove muffin molds from air fryer and add 2 tsp cheese mixture in the center of each egg cup.
7. Return muffin molds to the air fryer and cook for 10 minutes more.
8. Serve and enjoy.

Nutritional Value (Amount per Serving):

- Calories 225
- Fat 19 g
- Carbohydrates 1 g
- Sugar 0.4 g
- Protein 11 g
- Cholesterol 180 mg

Broccoli Muffins

Preparation Time: 10 minutes
Cooking Time: 24 minutes
Serve: 6

Ingredients:

- 2 large eggs
- 1 cup broccoli florets, chopped
- 1 cup unsweetened almond milk
- 2 cups almond flour
- 1 tsp baking powder
- 2 tbsp nutritional yeast
- 1/2 tsp sea salt

Directions:

1. Preheat the air fryer to 325 F.
2. Add all ingredients into the large bowl and mix until well combined.
3. Pour mixture into the silicone muffin molds and place into the air fryer basket.
4. Cook muffins for 20-24 minutes.
5. Serve and enjoy.

Nutritional Value (Amount per Serving):

- Calories 260
- Fat 21.2 g
- Carbohydrates 11 g
- Sugar 1.7 g
- Protein 12 g
- Cholesterol 62 mg

Asparagus Frittata

Preparation Time: 10 minutes
Cooking Time: 10 minutes
Serve: 4

Ingredients:

- 6 eggs
- 3 mushrooms, sliced
- 10 asparagus, chopped
- 1/4 cup half and half
- 2 tsp butter, melted
- 1 cup mozzarella cheese, shredded
- 1 tsp pepper
- 1 tsp salt

Directions:

1. Toss mushrooms and asparagus with melted butter and add into the air fryer basket.
2. Cook mushrooms and asparagus at 350 F for 5 minutes. Shake basket twice.
3. Meanwhile, in a bowl, whisk together eggs, half and half, pepper, and salt.
4. Transfer cook mushrooms and asparagus into the air fryer baking dish.
5. Pour egg mixture over mushrooms and asparagus.
6. Place dish in the air fryer and cook at 350 F for 5 minutes or until eggs are set.
7. Slice and serve.

Nutritional Value (Amount per Serving):

- Calories 211
- Fat 13 g
- Carbohydrates 4 g
- Sugar 1 g
- Protein 16 g
- Cholesterol 272 mg

Tomato Mushroom Mix

Preparation Time: 10 minutes
Cooking Time: 15 minutes
Serve: 4

Ingredients:

- 6 oz tomatoes, chopped
- 2 tbsp olive oil
- ½ tsp ground nutmeg
- 1 onion, chopped
- 15 oz mushrooms, sliced
- Pepper
- Salt

Directions:

1. Add all ingredients into the air fryer baking dish and mix well.
2. Place dish in the air fryer and cook at 380 F for 15 minutes.
3. Serve and enjoy.

Nutritional Value (Amount per Serving):

- Calories 103
- Fat 7.5 g
- Carbohydrates 7.9 g
- Sugar 4 g
- Protein 4 g
- Cholesterol 0 mg

Italian Chicken

Preparation Time: 10 minutes
Cooking Time: 20 minutes
Serve: 4

Ingredients:

- 4 chicken thighs
- ¼ tsp onion powder
- ½ tsp garlic powder
- 2 ½ tsp dried Italian herbs
- 2 tbsp butter, melted

Directions:

1. Brush chicken with melted butter.
2. Mix together Italian herbs, onion powder, and garlic powder and rub over chicken.
3. Place chicken into the air fryer basket and cook at 380 F for 20 minutes.
4. Serve and enjoy.

Nutritional Value (Amount per Serving):

- Calories 330
- Fat 16 g
- Carbohydrates 0.4 g
- Sugar 0.1 g
- Protein 42 g
- Cholesterol 145 mg

Healthy Squash

Preparation Time: 10 minutes
Cooking Time: 25 minutes
Serve: 4

Ingredients:

- 2 lbs yellow squash, cut into half-moons
- 1 tsp Italian seasoning
- ¼ tsp pepper
- 1 tbsp olive oil
- ¼ tsp salt

Directions:

1. Add all ingredients into the large bowl and toss well.
2. Preheat the air fryer to 400 F.
3. Add squash mixture into the air fryer basket and cook for 10 minutes.
4. Shake basket and cook for another 10 minutes.
5. Shake once again and cook for 5 minutes more.

Nutritional Value (Amount per Serving):

- Calories 70
- Fat 4 g
- Carbohydrates 7 g
- Sugar 4 g
- Protein 2 g
- Cholesterol 1 mg

Breakfast Egg Tomato

Preparation Time: 10 minutes
Cooking Time: 24 minutes
Serve: 2

Ingredients:

- 2 eggs
- 2 large fresh tomatoes
- 1 tsp fresh parsley
- Pepper
- Salt

Directions:

1. Preheat the air fryer to 325 F.
2. Cut off the top of a tomato and spoon out the tomato innards.
3. Break the egg in each tomato and place in air fryer basket and cook for 24 minutes.
4. Season with parsley, pepper, and salt.
5. Serve and enjoy.

Nutritional Value (Amount per Serving):

- Calories 95
- Fat 5 g
- Carbohydrates 7.5 g
- Sugar 5.1 g
- Protein 7 g
- Cholesterol 164 mg

Spinach Frittata

Preparation Time: 5 minutes
Cooking Time: 8 minutes
Serve: 1

Ingredients:

- 3 eggs
- 1 cup spinach, chopped
- 1 small onion, minced
- 2 tbsp mozzarella cheese, grated
- Pepper
- Salt

Directions:

1. Preheat the air fryer to 350 F.
2. Spray air fryer pan with cooking spray.
3. In a bowl, whisk eggs with remaining ingredients until well combined.
4. Pour egg mixture into the prepared pan and place pan in the air fryer basket.
5. Cook frittata for 8 minutes or until set.
6. Serve and enjoy.

Nutritional Value (Amount per Serving):

- Calories 384
- Fat 23.3 g
- Carbohydrates 10.7 g
- Sugar 4.1 g
- Protein 34.3 g
- Cholesterol 521 mg

Zucchini Squash Mix

Preparation Time: 10 minutes
Cooking Time: 35 minutes
Serve: 4

Ingredients:

- 1 lb zucchini, sliced
- 1 tbsp parsley, chopped
- 1 yellow squash, halved, deseeded, and chopped
- 1 tbsp olive oil
- Pepper
- Salt

Directions:

1. Add all ingredients into the large bowl and mix well.
2. Transfer bowl mixture into the air fryer basket and cook at 400 F for 35 minutes.
3. Serve and enjoy.

Nutritional Value (Amount per Serving):

- Calories 49
- Fat 3 g
- Carbohydrates 4 g
- Sugar 2 g
- Protein 1.5 g
- Cholesterol 0 mg

Zucchini Cheese Quiche

Preparation Time: 10 minutes
Cooking Time: 35 minutes
Serve: 6

Ingredients:

- 8 eggs
- 1 cup zucchini, shredded and squeezed
- 1 cup ham, cooked and diced
- 1/2 tsp dry mustard
- 1/2 cup heavy cream
- 1 cup cheddar cheese, shredded
- Pepper
- Salt

Directions:

1. Preheat the air fryer to 350 F.
2. Spray air fryer baking dish with cooking spray.
3. Combine ham, cheddar cheese, and zucchini in a baking dish.
4. In a bowl, whisk together eggs, heavy cream, and seasoning. Pour egg mixture over ham mixture.
5. Place dish in the air fryer and cook for 30-35 minutes.
6. Serve and enjoy.

Nutritional Value (Amount per Serving):

- Calories 234
- Fat 17 g
- Carbohydrates 2.5 g
- Sugar 1 g
- Protein 16 g
- Cholesterol 265 mg

Lemon Dill Scallops

Preparation Time: 10 minutes
Cooking Time: 5 minutes
Serve: 4

Ingredients:

- 1 lb scallops
- 2 tsp olive oil
- 1 tsp dill, chopped
- 1 tbsp fresh lemon juice
- Pepper
- Salt

Directions:

1. Add scallops into the bowl and toss with oil, dill, lemon juice, pepper, and salt.
2. Add scallops into the air fryer basket and cook at 360 F for 5 minutes.
3. Serve and enjoy.

Nutritional Value (Amount per Serving):

- Calories 121
- Fat 3.2 g
- Carbohydrates 2.9 g
- Sugar 0.1 g
- Protein 19 g
- Cholesterol 37 mg

Almond Pesto Salmon

Preparation Time: 10 minutes
Cooking Time: 12 minutes
Serve: 2

Ingredients:
- 2 salmon fillets
- 2 tbsp butter, melted
- ¼ cup pesto
- ¼ cup almond, ground

Directions:
1. Mix together pesto and almond.
2. Brush salmon fillets with melted butter and place into the air fryer baking dish.
3. Top salmon fillets with pesto and almond mixture.
4. Place dish in the air fryer and cook at 390 F for 12 minutes.
5. Serve and enjoy.

Nutritional Value (Amount per Serving):
- Calories 541
- Fat 41 g
- Carbohydrates 4 g
- Sugar 2.5 g
- Protein 40 g
- Cholesterol 117 mg

Shrimp Stuff Peppers

Preparation Time: 10 minutes
Cooking Time: 6 minutes
Serve: 6

Ingredients:

- 12 baby bell peppers, cut into halves
- 1 tbsp olive oil
- 1 tbsp fresh lemon juice
- ¼ cup basil pesto
- 1 lb shrimp, cooked
- ½ tsp red pepper flakes, crushed
- 2 tbsp parsley, chopped
- Pepper
- Salt

Directions:

1. In a bowl, mix together shrimp, parsley, red pepper flakes, basil pesto, lemon juice, oil, pepper, and salt.
2. Stuff shrimp mixture into the bell pepper halved and place into the air fryer basket.
3. Cook at 320 F for 6 minutes.
4. Serve and enjoy.

Nutritional Value (Amount per Serving):

- Calories 191
- Fat 3.7 g
- Carbohydrates 13 g
- Sugar 12 g
- Protein 19 g
- Cholesterol 159 mg

Delicious Eggplant Hash

Preparation Time: 10 minutes
Cooking Time: 14 minutes
Serve: 4

Ingredients:

- 1 eggplant, chopped
- ¼ cup fresh mint, chopped
- ¼ cup basil, chopped
- 1 tsp Tabasco sauce
- ½ lb cherry tomatoes halved
- ½ cup olive oil
- Pepper
- Salt

Directions:

1. Heat oil in a pan over medium-high heat.
2. Add eggplant into the pan and cook for 3 minutes stir well and cook for 3 minutes more.
3. Transfer eggplant into the air fryer baking dish.
4. Add tomatoes in the same pan and cook for 1-2 minutes.
5. Transfer tomatoes in eggplant dish along with remaining ingredients and stir well.
6. Place dish in the air fryer and cook at 320 F for 6 minutes.
7. Serve and enjoy.

Nutritional Value (Amount per Serving):

- Calories 258
- Fat 25 g
- Carbohydrates 9 g
- Sugar 4 g
- Protein 2 g
- Cholesterol 0 mg

Cheese Stuff Peppers

Preparation Time: 5 minutes
Cooking Time: 8 minutes
Serve: 8

Ingredients:

- 8 small bell pepper, cut the top of peppers
- 3.5 oz feta cheese, cubed
- 1 tbsp olive oil
- 1 tsp Italian seasoning
- 1 tbsp parsley, chopped
- ¼ tsp garlic powder
- Pepper
- Salt

Directions:

1. In a bowl, toss cheese with oil and seasoning.
2. Stuff cheese in each bell peppers and place into the air fryer basket.
3. Cook at 400 F for 8 minutes.
4. Serve and enjoy.

Nutritional Value (Amount per Serving):

- Calories 88
- Fat 5 g
- Carbohydrates 9 g
- Sugar 6 g
- Protein 3 g
- Cholesterol 10 mg

Almond Crust Chicken

Preparation Time: 10 minutes
Cooking Time: 25 minutes
Serve: 2

Ingredients:
- 2 chicken breasts, skinless and boneless
- 1 tbsp Dijon mustard
- 2 tbsp mayonnaise
- ¼ cup almonds
- Pepper
- Salt

Directions:
1. Add almond into the food processor and process until finely ground. Transfer almonds on a plate and set aside.
2. Mix together mustard and mayonnaise and spread over chicken.
3. Coat chicken with almond and place into the air fryer basket and cook at 350 F for 25 minutes.
4. Serve and enjoy.

Nutritional Value (Amount per Serving):
- Calories 409
- Fat 22 g
- Carbohydrates 6 g
- Sugar 1.5 g
- Protein 45 g
- Cholesterol 134 mg

Spicy Cauliflower Rice

Preparation Time: 10 minutes
Cooking Time: 22 minutes
Serve: 2

Ingredients:

- 1 cauliflower head, cut into florets
- 1/2 tsp cumin
- 1/2 tsp chili powder
- 6 onion spring, chopped
- 2 jalapenos, chopped
- 4 tbsp olive oil
- 1 zucchini, trimmed and cut into cubes
- 1/2 tsp paprika
- 1/2 tsp garlic powder
- 1/2 tsp cayenne pepper
- 1/2 tsp pepper
- 1/2 tsp salt

Directions:

1. Preheat the air fryer to 370 F.
2. Add cauliflower florets into the food processor and process until it looks like rice.
3. Transfer cauliflower rice into the air fryer baking pan and drizzle with half oil.
4. Place pan in the air fryer and cook for 12 minutes, stir halfway through.
5. Heat remaining oil in a small pan over medium heat.
6. Add zucchini and cook for 5-8 minutes.
7. Add onion and jalapenos and cook for 5 minutes.
8. Add spices and stir well. Set aside.
9. Add cauliflower rice in the zucchini mixture and stir well.
10. Serve and enjoy.

Nutritional Value (Amount per Serving):

- Calories 254
- Fat 28 g
- Carbohydrates 12.3 g
- Sugar 5 g
- Protein 4.3 g
- Cholesterol 0 mg

Chapter 5: Poultry Recipes

Turkey Meatballs

Preparation Time: 10 minutes
Cooking Time: 12 minutes
Serve: 4

Ingredients:

- 1 lb ground turkey
- 2 garlic cloves, minced
- ¼ cup carrots, grated
- 1 egg, lightly beaten
- 2 tbsp coconut flour
- 2 green onion, chopped
- ¼ cup celery, chopped
- Pepper
- Salt

Directions:

1. Spray air fryer basket with cooking spray.
2. Preheat the air fryer to 400 F.
3. Add all ingredients into the large bowl and mix until well combined.
4. Make balls from meat mixture and place into the air fryer basket and cook for 12 minutes. Turn halfway through.
5. Serve and enjoy.

Nutritional Value (Amount per Serving):

- Calories 275
- Fat 13 g
- Carbohydrates 6 g
- Sugar 1 g
- Protein 34 g
- Cholesterol 125 mg

Mediterranean Chicken

Preparation Time: 10 minutes
Cooking Time: 35 minutes
Serve: 6

Ingredients:

- 4 lbs whole chicken, cut into pieces
- 2 tsp ground sumac
- 2 garlic cloves, minced
- 2 lemons, sliced
- 2 tbsp olive oil
- 1 tsp lemon zest
- 2 tsp kosher salt

Directions:

1. Rub chicken with oil, sumac, lemon zest, and salt. Place in the refrigerator for 2-3 hours.
2. Add lemon sliced into the air fryer basket top with marinated chicken.
3. Cook at 350 for 35 minutes.
4. Serve and enjoy.

Nutritional Value (Amount per Serving):

- Calories 616
- Fat 27 g
- Carbohydrates 0.4 g
- Sugar 0 g
- Protein 87 g
- Cholesterol 269 mg

Quick & Simple Chicken Breast

Preparation Time: 10 minutes
Cooking Time: 22 minutes
Serve: 4

Ingredients:

- 4 chicken breasts, skinless and boneless
- 1/2 tsp dried oregano
- 1/2 tsp dried basil
- 1/2 tsp dried thyme
- 1/2 tsp garlic powder
- 2 tbsp olive oil
- 1/8 tsp pepper
- 1/2 tsp salt

Directions:

1. In a small bowl, mix together olive oil, oregano, basil, thyme, garlic powder, pepper, and salt.
2. Rub herb oil mixture all over chicken breasts.
3. Spray air fryer basket with cooking spray.
4. Place chicken in air fryer basket and cook at 360 F for 10 minutes.
5. Turn chicken to another side and cook for 8-12 minutes more or until the internal temperature of chicken reaches at 165 F.
6. Serve and enjoy.

Nutritional Value (Amount per Serving):

- Calories 340
- Fat 17.9 g
- Carbohydrates 0.5 g
- Sugar 0.1 g
- Protein 42.3 g
- Cholesterol 130 mg

Teriyaki Chicken

Preparation Time: 10 minutes
Cooking Time: 20 minutes
Serve: 6

Ingredients:

- 6 chicken drumsticks
- 1 cup keto teriyaki sauce
- 1 tbsp sesame seeds, toasted
- 2 tbsp green onion, sliced

Directions:

1. Add chicken and teriyaki sauce into the large zip-lock bag. Shake well and place in the refrigerator for 1 hour.
2. Preheat the air fryer to 360 F.
3. Add marinated chicken drumsticks into the air fryer basket and cook for 20 minutes. Shake basket twice.
4. Garnish with green onion and sesame seeds.
5. Serve and enjoy.

Nutritional Value (Amount per Serving):

- Calories 165
- Fat 7 g
- Carbohydrates 7 g
- Sugar 6 g
- Protein 16 g
- Cholesterol 65 mg

Lemon Pepper Chicken Wings

Preparation Time: 10 minutes
Cooking Time: 16 minutes
Serve: 4

Ingredients:

- 1 lb chicken wings
- 1 tsp lemon pepper
- 1 tbsp olive oil
- 1 tsp salt

Directions:

1. Add chicken wings into the large mixing bowl.
2. Add remaining ingredients over chicken and toss well to coat.
3. Place chicken wings in the air fryer basket.
4. Cook chicken wings for 8 minutes at 400 F.
5. Turn chicken wings to another side and cook for 8 minutes more.
6. Serve and enjoy.

Nutritional Value (Amount per Serving):

- Calories 247
- Fat 11 g
- Carbohydrates 0.3 g
- Sugar 0 g
- Protein 32 g
- Cholesterol 101 mg

Asain Chicken Wings

Preparation Time: 10 minutes
Cooking Time: 30 minutes
Serve: 2

Ingredients:

- 4 chicken wings
- 3/4 tbsp Chinese spice
- 1 tbsp soy sauce
- 1 tsp mixed spice
- Pepper
- Salt

Directions:

1. Add chicken wings into the bowl. Add remaining ingredients and toss to coat.
2. Transfer chicken wings into the air fryer basket.
3. Cook at 350 f for 15 minutes
4. Turn chicken to another side and cook for 15 minutes more.
5. Serve and enjoy.

Nutritional Value (Amount per Serving):

- Calories 560
- Fat 21 g
- Carbohydrates 0.5 g
- Sugar 0.2 g
- Protein 86 g
- Cholesterol 134 mg

Chicken Fajita Casserole

Preparation Time: 10 minutes
Cooking Time: 12 minutes
Serve: 4

Ingredients:

- 1 lb cooked chicken, shredded
- 1 onion, sliced
- 1 bell pepper, sliced
- 1/3 cup mayonnaise
- 7 oz cream cheese
- 7 oz cheese, shredded
- 2 tbsp tex-mex seasoning
- Pepper
- Salt

Directions:

1. Preheat the air fryer to 370 F.
2. Spray air fryer baking dish with cooking spray.
3. Mix all ingredients except 2 oz shredded cheese in a prepared dish.
4. Spread remaining cheese on top.
5. Place dish in the air fryer and cook for 12 minutes.
6. Serve and enjoy.

Nutritional Value (Amount per Serving):

- Calories 640
- Fat 43.8 g
- Carbohydrates 11 g
- Sugar 4.3 g
- Protein 50 g
- Cholesterol 200 mg

Dijon Turkey Drumstick

Preparation Time: 10 minutes
Cooking Time: 28 minutes
Serve: 2

Ingredients:

- 4 turkey drumsticks
- 1/3 tsp paprika
- 1/3 cup sherry wine
- 1/3 cup coconut milk
- 1/2 tbsp ginger, minced
- 2 tbsp Dijon mustard
- Pepper
- Salt

Directions:

1. Add all ingredients into the large bowl and stir to coat. Place in refrigerator for 2 hours.
2. Spray air fryer basket with cooking spray.
3. Place marinated turkey drumsticks into the air fryer basket and cook at 380 F for 28 minutes. Turn halfway through.
4. Serve and enjoy.

Nutritional Value (Amount per Serving):

- Calories 365
- Fat 18 g
- Carbohydrates 5 g
- Sugar 2 g
- Protein 40 g
- Cholesterol 0 mg

Quick & Easy Meatballs

Preparation Time: 10 minutes
Cooking Time: 10 minutes
Serve: 4

Ingredients:

- 1 lb ground chicken
- 1 egg, lightly beaten
- 1/2 cup mozzarella cheese, shredded
- 1 1/2 tbsp taco seasoning
- 3 garlic cloves, minced
- 3 tbsp fresh parsley, chopped
- 1 small onion, minced
- Pepper
- Salt

Directions:

1. Add all ingredients into the large mixing bowl and mix until well combined.
2. Make small balls from mixture and place in the air fryer basket.
3. Cook meatballs for 10 minutes at 400 F.
4. Serve and enjoy.

Nutritional Value (Amount per Serving):

- Calories 253
- Fat 10 g
- Carbohydrates 2 g
- Sugar 0.9 g
- Protein 35 g
- Cholesterol 144 mg

Easy & Spicy Chicken Wings

Preparation Time: 10 minutes
Cooking Time: 25 minutes
Serve: 2

Ingredients:

- 1 lb chicken wings
- 1/2 tsp pepper
- 1/2 tsp salt
- For sauce:
- 1/2 tbsp sesame oil
- 1/2 tbsp mayonnaise
- 1 tbsp gochujang
- 1/2 tbsp garlic, minced
- 1.2 tbsp ginger, minced

Directions:

1. Preheat the air fryer to 400 F.
2. Add chicken wings into the air fryer basket and season with pepper and salt and cook for 20 minutes.
3. Meanwhile, in a bowl mix together all sauce ingredients.
4. Toss chicken wings with sauce and cook for 5 minutes more.
5. Serve and enjoy.

Nutritional Value (Amount per Serving):

- Calories 505
- Fat 22 g
- Carbohydrates 7 g
- Sugar 4 g
- Protein 66.1 g
- Cholesterol 200 mg

Delicious Chicken Fajitas

Preparation Time: 10 minutes
Cooking Time: 15 minutes
Serve: 4

Ingredients:

- 4 chicken breasts
- 1 onion, sliced
- 1 bell pepper, sliced
- 1 1/2 tbsp fajita seasoning
- 2 tbsp olive oil
- 3/4 cup cheddar cheese, shredded

Directions:

1. Preheat the air fryer at 380 F.
2. Coat chicken with oil and rub with seasoning.
3. Place chicken into the air fryer baking dish and top with bell peppers and onion.
4. Cook for 15 minutes.
5. Top with shredded cheese and cook for 1-2 minutes until cheese is melted.
6. Serve and enjoy.

Nutritional Value (Amount per Serving):

- Calories 425
- Fat 23 g
- Carbohydrates 7 g
- Sugar 2 g
- Protein 45 g
- Cholesterol 142 mg

Pesto Chicken

Preparation Time: 10 minutes
Cooking Time: 20 minutes
Serve: 2

Ingredients:

- 4 chicken drumsticks
- 6 garlic cloves
- 1/2 jalapeno pepper
- 2 tbsp lemon juice
- 2 tbsp olive oil
- 1 tbsp ginger, sliced
- 1/2 cup cilantro
- 1 tsp salt

Directions:

1. Add all the ingredients except chicken into the blender and blend until smooth.
2. Pour blended mixture into the large bowl.
3. Add chicken and stir well to coat. Place in refrigerator for 2 hours.
4. Spray air fryer basket with cooking spray.
5. Place marinated chicken into the air fryer basket and cook at 390 F for 20 minutes. Turn halfway through.
6. Serve and enjoy.

Nutritional Value (Amount per Serving):

- Calories 305
- Fat 19 g
- Carbohydrates 5 g
- Sugar 0.7 g
- Protein 25 g
- Cholesterol 80 mg

Thyme Butter Turkey Breast

Preparation Time: 10 minutes
Cooking Time: 60 minutes
Serve: 8

Ingredients:
- 2 lbs turkey breast
- ½ tsp thyme leaves, chopped
- ¼ tsp pepper
- ½ tsp sage leaves, chopped
- 1 tbsp butter
- 1 tsp salt

Directions:
1. Spray air fryer basket with cooking spray.
2. Rub butter all over the turkey breast and season with pepper, sage, thyme, and salt.
3. Place turkey breast into the air fryer basket and cook at 25 F for 60 minutes. Turn turkey breast to another side halfway through.
4. Slice and serve.

Nutritional Value (Amount per Serving):
- Calories 130
- Fat 3 g
- Carbohydrates 5 g
- Sugar 4 g
- Protein 19 g
- Cholesterol 145 mg

Korean Chicken Tenders

Preparation Time: 10 minutes
Cooking Time: 10 minutes
Serve: 3

Ingredients:

- 12 oz chicken tenders, skinless and boneless
- 2 tbsp green onion, chopped
- 3 garlic cloves, chopped
- 2 tsp sesame seeds, toasted
- 1 tbsp ginger, grated
- 1/4 cup sesame oil
- 1/2 cup soy sauce
- 1/4 tsp pepper

Directions:

1. Slide chicken tenders onto the skewers.
2. In a large bowl, mix together green onion, garlic, sesame seeds, ginger, sesame oil, soy sauce, and pepper.
3. Add chicken skewers into the bowl and coat well with marinade. Place in refrigerator for overnight.
4. Preheat the air fryer to 390 F.
5. Place marinated chicken skewers into the air fryer basket and cook for 10 minutes.

Nutritional Value (Amount per Serving):

- Calories 423
- Fat 27 g
- Carbohydrates 6 g
- Sugar 1 g
- Protein 36 g
- Cholesterol 101 mg

Garlic Herb Chicken Breasts

Preparation Time: 10 minutes
Cooking Time: 15 minutes
Serve: 5

Ingredients:

- 2 lbs chicken breasts, skinless and boneless
- 4 garlic cloves, minced
- ¼ cup yogurt
- ¼ cup mayonnaise
- 2 tsp garlic herb seasoning
- 1/2 tsp onion powder
- ¼ tsp salt

Directions:

1. Preheat the air fryer to 380 F.
2. In a small bowl, mix together mayonnaise, seasoning, onion powder, garlic, and yogurt.
3. Brush chicken with mayo mixture and season with salt.
4. Spray air fryer basket with cooking spray.
5. Place chicken into the air fryer basket and cook for 15 minutes.
6. Serve and enjoy.

Nutritional Value (Amount per Serving):

- Calories 410
- Fat 16 g
- Carbohydrates 5 g
- Sugar 2 g
- Protein 55 g
- Cholesterol 146 mg

Tasty Caribbean Chicken

Preparation Time: 10 minutes
Cooking Time: 10 minutes
Serve: 8

Ingredients:

- 3 lbs chicken thigh, skinless and boneless
- 1 tbsp coriander powder
- 3 tbsp coconut oil, melted
- ½ tsp ground nutmeg
- ½ tsp ground ginger
- 1 tbsp cayenne
- 1 tbsp cinnamon
- Pepper
- Salt

Directions:

1. In a small bowl, mix together all spices and rub all over the chicken.
2. Spray air fryer basket with cooking spray.
3. Place chicken into the air fryer basket and cook at 390 F for 10 minutes.
4. Serve and enjoy.

Nutritional Value (Amount per Serving):

- Calories 375
- Fat 18 g
- Carbohydrates 1 g
- Sugar 0.2 g
- Protein 50 g
- Cholesterol 142 mg

Juicy & Spicy Chicken Wings

Preparation Time: 10 minutes
Cooking Time: 25 minutes
Serve: 4

Ingredients:

- 2 lbs chicken wings
- 12 oz hot sauce
- 1 tsp Worcestershire sauce
- 1 tsp Tabasco
- 6 tbsp butter, melted

Directions:

1. Spray air fryer basket with cooking spray.
2. Add chicken wings into the air fryer basket and cook at 380 F for 25 minutes. Shake basket after every 5 minutes.
3. Meanwhile, in a bowl, mix together hot sauce, Worcestershire sauce, and butter. Set aside.
4. Add chicken wings into the sauce and toss well.
5. Serve and enjoy.

Nutritional Value (Amount per Serving):

- Calories 595
- Fat 35 g
- Carbohydrates 1 g
- Sugar 1 g
- Protein 65 g
- Cholesterol 142 mg

Indian Chicken Tenders

Preparation Time: 10 minutes
Cooking Time: 15 minutes
Serve: 4

Ingredients:

- 1 lb chicken tenders, cut in half
- ¼ cup parsley, chopped
- 1/2 tbsp garlic, minced
- 1/2 tbsp ginger, minced
- ¼ cup yogurt
- 3/4 tsp paprika
- 1 tsp garam masala
- 1 tsp turmeric
- 1/2 tsp cayenne pepper
- 1 tsp salt

Directions:

1. Preheat the air fryer to 350 F.
2. Add all ingredients into the large bowl and mix well. Place in refrigerator for 30 minutes.
3. Spray air fryer basket with cooking spray.
4. Add marinated chicken into the air fryer basket and cook for 10 minutes.
5. Turn chicken to another side and cook for 5 minutes more.
6. Serve and enjoy.

Nutritional Value (Amount per Serving):

- Calories 241
- Fat 10 g
- Carbohydrates 4 g
- Sugar 1 g
- Protein 35 g
- Cholesterol 24 mg

Curried Drumsticks

Preparation Time: 10 minutes
Cooking Time: 22 minutes
Serve: 2

Ingredients:

- 2 turkey drumsticks
- 1/3 cup coconut milk
- 1 1/2 tbsp ginger, minced
- 1/4 tsp cayenne pepper
- 2 tbsp red curry paste
- 1/4 tsp pepper
- 1 tsp kosher salt

Directions:

1. Add all ingredients into the bowl and stir to coat. Place in refrigerator for overnight.
2. Spray air fryer basket with cooking spray.
3. Place marinated drumsticks into the air fryer basket and cook at 390 F for 22 minutes.
4. Serve and enjoy.

Nutritional Value (Amount per Serving):

- Calories 279
- Fat 18 g
- Carbohydrates 8 g
- Sugar 1.5 g
- Protein 20 g
- Cholesterol 0 mg

Classic Chicken Wings

Preparation Time: 10 minutes
Cooking Time: 40 minutes
Serve: 4

Ingredients:

- 2 lbs chicken wings

For sauce:

- 1/4 tsp Tabasco
- 1/4 tsp Worcestershire sauce
- 6 tbsp butter, melted
- 12 oz hot sauce

Directions:

1. Spray air fryer basket with cooking spray.
2. Add chicken wings in air fryer basket and cook for 25 minutes at 380 F. Shake basket after every 5 minutes
3. After 25 minutes turn temperature to 400 F and cook for 10-15 minutes more.
4. Meanwhile, in a large bowl, mix together all sauce ingredients.
5. Add cooked chicken wings in a sauce bowl and toss well to coat.
6. Serve and enjoy.

Nutritional Value (Amount per Serving):

- Calories 593
- Fat 34.4 g
- Carbohydrates 1.6 g
- Sugar 1.1 g
- Protein 66.2 g
- Cholesterol 248 mg

Chapter 6: Beef Pork & Lamb Recipes

Simple Air Fryer Steak

Preparation Time: 10 minutes
Cooking Time: 18 minutes
Serve: 2

Ingredients:

- 12 oz steaks, 3/4-inch thick
- 1 tsp garlic powder
- 1 tsp olive oil
- Pepper
- Salt

Directions:

- Coat steaks with oil and season with garlic powder, pepper, and salt.
- Preheat the air fryer to 400 F.
- Place steaks in air fryer basket and cook for 15-18 minutes. Turn halfway through.
- Serve and enjoy.

Nutritional Value (Amount per Serving):

- Calories 363
- Carbohydrates 1.1 g
- Sugar 0.3 g
- Protein 61.7 g
- Cholesterol 153 mg

Beef Roast

Preparation Time: 10 minutes
Cooking Time: 35 minutes
Serve: 7

Ingredients:

- 2 lbs beef roast
- 1 tbsp olive oil
- 1 tsp thyme
- 2 tsp garlic powder
- 1/4 tsp pepper
- 1 tbsp kosher salt

Directions:

1. Coat roast with olive oil.
2. Mix together thyme, garlic powder, pepper, and salt and rub all over roast.
3. Place roast into the air fryer basket and cook at 400 F for 20 minutes.
4. Spray roast with cooking spray and cook for 15 minutes more.
5. Slice and serve.

Nutritional Value (Amount per Serving):

- Calories 238
- Fat 13 g
- Carbohydrates 1 g
- Sugar 0.5 g
- Protein 25 g
- Cholesterol 89 mg

Crisp Pork Chops

Preparation Time: 10 minutes
Cooking Time: 12 minutes
Serve: 6

Ingredients:

- 1 1/2 lbs pork chops, boneless
- 1 tsp paprika
- 1 tsp creole seasoning
- 1 tsp garlic powder
- 1/4 cup parmesan cheese, grated
- 1/3 cup almond flour

Directions:

1. Preheat the air fryer to 360 F.
2. Add all ingredients except pork chops in a zip-lock bag.
3. Add pork chops in the bag. Seal bag and shake well to coat pork chops.
4. Remove pork chops from zip-lock bag and place in the air fryer basket.
5. Cook pork chops for 10-12 minutes.
6. Serve and enjoy.

Nutritional Value (Amount per Serving):

- Calories 230
- Fat 11 g
- Carbohydrates 2 g
- Sugar 0.2 g
- Protein 27 g
- Cholesterol 79 mg

Lemon Mustard Lamb Chops

Preparation Time: 10 minutes
Cooking Time: 15 minutes
Serve: 4

Ingredients:

- 8 lamb chops
- 1 tbsp lemon juice
- 1 tsp tarragon
- 1/2 tsp olive oil
- 2 tbsp Dijon mustard
- Pepper
- Salt

Directions:

1. Preheat the air fryer to 390 F.
2. In a small bowl, mix together mustard, lemon juice, tarragon, and olive oil.
3. Brush mustard mixture over lamb chops.
4. Place lamb chops in air fryer basket and cook for 15 minutes. Turn halfway through.
5. Serve and enjoy.

Nutritional Value (Amount per Serving):

- Calories 328
- Fat 13.4 g
- Carbohydrates 0.6 g
- Sugar 0.2 g
- Protein 48.1 g
- Cholesterol 153 mg

Juicy & Tender Steak

Preparation Time: 10 minutes
Cooking Time: 12 minutes
Serve: 2

Ingredients:

- 2 rib-eye steak
- 3 tbsp fresh parsley, chopped
- 1 stick butter, softened
- 1 1/2 tsp Worcestershire sauce
- 3 garlic cloves, minced
- Pepper
- Salt

Directions:

1. In a bowl, mix together butter, Worcestershire sauce, garlic, parsley, and salt and place in the refrigerator.
2. Preheat the air fryer to 400 F.
3. Season steak with pepper and salt.
4. Place seasoned steak in the air fryer and cook for 12 minutes. Turn halfway through.
5. Remove steak from air fryer and top with butter mixture.
6. Serve and enjoy.

Nutritional Value (Amount per Serving):

- Calories 590
- Fat 57 g
- Carbohydrates 3 g
- Sugar 0.5 g
- Protein 16 g
- Cholesterol 423 mg

Lamb Meatballs

Preparation Time: 10 minutes
Cooking Time: 14 minutes
Serve: 8

Ingredients:

- 1 egg, lightly beaten
- 1 lb ground lamb
- ¼ tsp bay leaf, crushed
- 1 tsp ground coriander
- ¼ tsp cayenne pepper
- ¼ tsp turmeric
- 1 onion, chopped
- 2 garlic cloves, minced
- ¼ tsp pepper
- 1 tsp salt

Directions:

1. Preheat the air fryer to 400 F.
2. Spray air fryer basket with cooking spray.
3. Add all ingredients into the large bowl and mix until well combined.
4. Make small balls from meat mixture and place into the air fryer basket and cook for 14 minutes. Shake basket twice while cooking.
5. Serve and enjoy.

Nutritional Value (Amount per Serving):

- Calories 121
- Fat 4 g
- Carbohydrates 2 g
- Sugar 0.5 g
- Protein 16 g
- Cholesterol 70 mg

Steak Fajitas

Preparation Time: 10 minutes
Cooking Time: 15 minutes
Serve: 6

Ingredients:

- 1 lb steak, sliced
- 1 tbsp olive oil
- 1 tbsp fajita seasoning, gluten-free
- 1/2 cup onion, sliced
- 3 bell peppers, sliced

Directions:

1. Line air fryer basket with aluminum foil.
2. Add all ingredients large bowl and toss until well coated.
3. Transfer fajita mixture into the air fryer basket and cook at 390 F for 5 minutes.
4. Toss well and cook for 5-10 minutes more.
5. Serve and enjoy.

Nutritional Value (Amount per Serving):

- Calories 304
- Fat 17 g
- Carbohydrates 15 g
- Sugar 4 g
- Protein 22 g
- Cholesterol 73 mg

Asian Beef

Preparation Time: 10 minutes
Cooking Time: 20 minutes
Serve: 4

Ingredients:

- 1 lb beef tips, sliced
- 1/4 cup green onion, chopped
- 2 tbsp garlic, minced
- 2 tbsp sesame oil
- 1 tbsp fish sauce
- 2 tbsp coconut aminos
- 1 tsp xanthan gum
- 2 red chili peppers, sliced
- 2 tbsp water
- 1 tbsp ginger, sliced

Directions:

1. Spray air fryer basket with cooking spray.
2. Toss beef and xanthan gum together.
3. Add beef into the air fryer basket and cook at 390F for 20 minutes. Toss halfway through.
4. Meanwhile, in a saucepan add remaining ingredients except for green onion and heat over low heat.
5. When sauce begins to boiling then remove from heat.
6. Add cooked meat into the saucepan and stir to coat. Let sit in for 5 minutes.
7. Garnish with green onion and serve.

Nutritional Value (Amount per Serving):

- Calories 295
- Fat 15 g
- Carbohydrates 6 g
- Sugar 0.4 g
- Protein 35 g
- Cholesterol 42 mg

Pork Strips

Preparation Time: 10 minutes
Cooking Time: 10 minutes
Serve: 2

Ingredients:

- 4 pork loin chops
- 1 tbsp swerve
- 1 tbsp soy sauce
- 1/8 tsp ground ginger
- 1 garlic clove, chopped
- 1/2 tsp balsamic vinegar

Directions:

1. Tenderize meat and season with pepper and salt.
2. In a bowl, mix together sweetener, soy sauce, and vinegar. Add ginger and garlic and set aside.
3. Add pork chops into the marinade mixture and marinate for 2 hours.
4. Preheat the air fryer to 350 F.
5. Add marinated meat into the air fryer and cook for 5 minutes on each side.
6. Cut into strips and serve.

Nutritional Value (Amount per Serving):

- Calories 551
- Fat 39.8 g
- Carbohydrates 9.9 g
- Sugar 8.8 g
- Protein 36.6 g
- Cholesterol 138 mg

Meatloaf Sliders

Preparation Time: 10 minutes
Cooking Time: 10 minutes
Serve: 8

Ingredients:
- 1 lb ground beef
- 1/2 tsp dried tarragon
- 1 tsp Italian seasoning
- 1 tbsp Worcestershire sauce
- 1/4 cup ketchup
- 1/4 cup coconut flour
- 1/2 cup almond flour
- 1 garlic clove, minced
- 1/4 cup onion, chopped
- 2 eggs, lightly beaten
- 1/4 tsp pepper
- 1/2 tsp sea salt

Directions:
1. Add all ingredients into the mixing bowl and mix until well combined.
2. Make the equal shape of patties from mixture and place on a plate. Place in refrigerator for 10 minutes.
3. Spray air fryer basket with cooking spray.
4. Preheat the air fryer to 360 F.
5. Place prepared patties in air fryer basket and cook for 10 minutes.
6. Serve and enjoy.

Nutritional Value (Amount per Serving):
- Calories 228
- Fat 16 g
- Carbohydrates 6 g
- Sugar 2 g
- Protein 13 g
- Cholesterol 80 mg

Meatballs

Preparation Time: 10 minutes
Cooking Time: 8 minutes
Serve: 10

Ingredients:

- 5 oz ground beef
- 1 tbsp fresh oregano, chopped
- 2 oz feta cheese, crumbled
- 2 tbsp almond flour
- 1/4 tsp garlic powder
- 1/4 tsp paprika
- Pepper
- Salt

Directions:

1. Preheat the air fryer to 390 F.
2. Add all ingredients into the bowl and mix until well combined.
3. Make small balls from meat mixture and place into the air fryer basket.
4. Cook for 8 minutes.
5. Serve and enjoy.

Nutritional Value (Amount per Serving):

- Calories 75
- Fat 4 g
- Carbohydrates 2 g
- Sugar 0.6 g
- Protein 7 g
- Cholesterol 65 mg

Broccoli Beef

Preparation Time: 10 minutes
Cooking Time: 12 minutes
Serve: 5

Ingredients:

- 1 lb round steak, cut into strips
- 1 lb broccoli florets
- 5 drops liquid stevia
- 1 tsp soy sauce
- 1/3 cup sherry
- 2 tsp sesame oil
- 1/3 cup oyster sauce
- 1 garlic clove, minced
- 1 tbsp ginger, sliced
- 1 tsp arrowroot powder
- 1 tbsp olive oil

Directions:

1. In a small bowl, combine together oyster sauce, stevia, soy sauce, sherry, arrowroot, and sesame oil.
2. Add broccoli and meat in a large bowl.
3. Pour oyster sauce mixture over meat and broccoli and toss well. Place in the fridge for 60 minutes.
4. Add marinated meat broccoli to the air fryer basket. Drizzle with olive oil and sprinkle with ginger and garlic.
5. Cook at 360 F for 12 minutes.
6. Serve and enjoy.

Nutritional Value (Amount per Serving):

- Calories 302
- Fat 20 g
- Carbohydrates 8 g
- Sugar 2 g
- Protein 24 g
- Cholesterol 142 mg

Sweet Mustard Pork Chops

Preparation Time: 10 minutes
Cooking Time: 12 minutes
Serve: 2

Ingredients:

- 1/2 lb pork chops, boneless
- 1 tbsp Swerve
- 1/2 tsp steak seasoning blend
- 1/2 tbsp mustard

Directions:

1. In a small bowl, mix together steak seasoning, swerve, and mustard.
2. Rub steak seasoning mixture over pork chops and place into the air fryer basket.
3. Cook at 350 F for 12 minutes. Turn halfway through.
4. Serve and enjoy.

Nutritional Value (Amount per Serving):

- Calories 395
- Fat 27 g
- Carbohydrates 9 g
- Sugar 8 g
- Protein 24 g
- Cholesterol 95 mg

Asian Pork

Preparation Time: 10 minutes
Cooking Time: 15 minutes
Serve: 4

Ingredients:

- 1 lb pork shoulder, boneless and cut into 1/2 inch sliced
- 3 tbsp green onions, sliced
- 3 garlic cloves, minced
- 1 tbsp ginger, minced
- 2 tbsp red pepper paste
- 1 onion, sliced
- 1 tbsp sesame seeds
- 3/4 tsp cayenne pepper
- 1 tbsp sesame oil
- 1 tbsp rice wine

Directions:

1. Add all ingredients into the bowl and mix well and place in the refrigerator for 1 hour.
2. Place marinated meat and onion slices into the air fryer.
3. Cook at 400 F for 15 minutes. Toss halfway through.
4. Serve and enjoy.

Nutritional Value (Amount per Serving):

- Calories 405
- Fat 30 g
- Carbohydrates 8 g
- Sugar 3 g
- Protein 30 g
- Cholesterol 105 mg

Garlic Pork Chops

Preparation Time: 5 minutes
Cooking Time: 20 minutes
Serve: 5

Ingredients:

- 2 lbs pork chops
- 2 tbsp garlic, minced
- 1 tbsp fresh parsley
- 2 tbsp olive oil
- 2 tbsp fresh lemon juice
- Pepper
- Salt

Directions:

1. In a small bowl, mix together garlic, parsley, oil, and lemon juice.
2. Season pork chops with pepper and salt.
3. Rub garlic mixture over the pork chops and allow to marinate for 30 minutes.
4. Add marinated pork chops into the air fryer and cook at 400 F for 10 minutes.
5. Turn pork chops to another side and cook for 10 minutes more.
6. Serve and enjoy.

Nutritional Value (Amount per Serving):

- Calories 625
- Fat 50 g
- Carbohydrates 2 g
- Sugar 0.5 g
- Protein 40 g
- Cholesterol 124 mg

Perfect Cheeseburger

Preparation Time: 5 minutes
Cooking Time: 12 minutes
Serve: 2

Ingredients:

- 1/2 lb ground beef
- 1/4 tsp onion powder
- 2 cheese slices
- 1/4 tsp pepper
- 1/8 tsp salt

Directions:

1. In a bowl, mix together ground beef, onion powder, pepper, and salt.
2. Make two equal shapes of patties from meat mixture and place in the air fryer basket.
3. Cook patties at 370 F for 12 minutes. Turn patties halfway through.
4. Once air fryer timer goes off then place cheese slices on top of each patty and close the air fryer basket for 1 minute.
5. Serve and enjoy.

Nutritional Value (Amount per Serving):

- Calories 325
- Fat 16.4 g
- Carbohydrates 0.8 g
- Sugar 0.3 g
- Protein 41.4 g
- Cholesterol 131 mg

Lamb Rack

Preparation Time: 10 minutes
Cooking Time: 30 minutes
Serve: 6

Ingredients:

- 1 egg, lightly beaten
- 1 tbsp fresh thyme, chopped
- 1 3/4 lbs rack of lamb
- 1 tbsp fresh rosemary, chopped
- 1 tbsp olive oil
- 2 garlic cloves, chopped
- Pepper
- Salt

Directions:

1. Mix together oil and garlic.
2. Brush oil and garlic mixture over the rack of lamb. Season with pepper and salt.
3. Preheat the air fryer to 210 F.
4. Mix together thyme and rosemary.
5. Coat lamb with egg then with herb mixture.
6. Place lamb rack in the air fryer basket and cook for 25 minutes.
7. Turn temperature to 390 F and cook for 5 minutes more.
8. Serve and enjoy.

Nutritional Value (Amount per Serving):

- Calories 255
- Fat 15 g
- Carbohydrates 1 g
- Sugar 0.3 g
- Protein 29 g
- Cholesterol 114 mg

Jerk Pork

Preparation Time: 10 minutes
Cooking Time: 20 minutes
Serve: 4

Ingredients:

- 1 1/2 lbs pork butt, chopped into pieces
- 3 tbsp jerk paste

Directions:

1. Add meat and jerk paste into the bowl and coat well. Place in the fridge for overnight.
2. Spray air fryer basket with cooking spray.
3. Preheat the air fryer to 390 F.
4. Add marinated meat into the air fryer and cook for 20 minutes. Turn halfway through.
5. Serve and enjoy.

Nutritional Value (Amount per Serving):

- Calories 325
- Fat 12 g
- Carbohydrates 0.5 g
- Sugar 0 g
- Protein 52 g
- Cholesterol 124 mg

Meatloaf

Preparation Time: 10 minutes
Cooking Time: 15 minutes
Serve: 4

Ingredients:

- 1 lb ground beef
- 1/4 tsp cinnamon
- 1 tbsp ginger, minced
- 1/4 cup fresh cilantro, chopped
- 1 cup onion, diced
- 2 eggs, lightly beaten
- 1 tsp cayenne
- 1 tsp turmeric
- 1 tsp garam masala
- 1 tbsp garlic, minced
- 1 tsp salt

Directions:

1. Add all ingredients into the large bowl and mix until combined.
2. Transfer meat mixture into the silicone meatloaf pan.
3. Place in the air fryer and cook at 360 F for 15 minutes.
4. Slice and serve.

Nutritional Value (Amount per Serving):

- Calories 260
- Fat 10 g
- Carbohydrates 4 g
- Sugar 2 g
- Protein 38 g
- Cholesterol 25 mg

Easy Burger Patties

Preparation Time: 10 minutes
Cooking Time: 45 minutes
Serve: 4

Ingredients:

- 10 oz ground beef
- 1 tsp dried basil
- 1 tsp mustard
- 1 tsp tomato paste
- 1 oz cheddar cheese
- 1 tsp mixed herbs
- 1 tsp garlic puree
- Pepper
- Salt

Directions:

1. Add all ingredients into the large bowl and mix until combined.
2. Spray air fryer basket with cooking spray.
3. Make patties from meat mixture and place into the air fryer basket.
4. Cook at 390 F for 25 minutes then turn patties to another side and cook at 350 F for 20 minutes more.
5. Serve and enjoy.

Nutritional Value (Amount per Serving):

- Calories 175
- Fat 7 g
- Carbohydrates 1 g
- Sugar 2 g
- Protein 25 g
- Cholesterol 125 mg

Chapter 7: Seafood & Fish Recipes

Shrimp with Veggie

Preparation Time: 10 minutes
Cooking Time: 20 minutes
Serve: 4

Ingredients:

- 50 small shrimp
- 1 tbsp Cajun seasoning
- 1 bag of frozen mix vegetables
- 1 tbsp olive oil

Directions:

1. Line air fryer basket with aluminum foil.
2. Add all ingredients into the large mixing bowl and toss well.
3. Transfer shrimp and vegetable mixture into the air fryer basket and cook at 350 F for 10 minutes.
4. Toss well and cook for 10 minutes more.
5. Serve and enjoy.

Nutritional Value (Amount per Serving):

- Calories 101
- Fat 4 g
- Carbohydrates 14 g
- Sugar 1 g
- Protein 2 g
- Cholesterol 3 mg

Salmon Patties

Preparation Time: 10 minutes
Cooking Time: 7 minutes
Serve: 2

Ingredients:

- 8 oz salmon fillet, minced
- 1 lemon, sliced
- 1/2 tsp garlic powder
- 1 egg, lightly beaten
- 1/8 tsp salt

Directions:

1. Add all ingredients except lemon slices into the bowl and mix until well combined.
2. Spray air fryer basket with cooking spray.
3. Place lemon slice into the air fryer basket.
4. Make the equal shape of patties from salmon mixture and place on top of lemon slices into the air fryer basket.
5. Cook at 390 F for 7 minutes.
6. Serve and enjoy.

Nutritional Value (Amount per Serving):

- Calories 184
- Fat 9.2 g
- Carbohydrates 1 g
- Sugar 0.4 g
- Protein 24.9 g
- Cholesterol 132 mg

Pesto Salmon

Preparation Time: 10 minutes
Cooking Time: 16 minutes
Serve: 2

Ingredients:

- 2 salmon fillets
- 1/4 cup parmesan cheese, grated
- For pesto:
- 1/4 cup pine nuts
- 1/4 cup olive oil
- 1 1/2 cups fresh basil leaves
- 2 garlic cloves, peeled and chopped
- 1/4 cup parmesan cheese, grated
- 1/2 tsp pepper
- 1/2 tsp salt

Directions:

1. Add all pesto ingredients to the blender and blend until smooth.
2. Preheat the air fryer to 370 F.
3. Spray air fryer basket with cooking spray.
4. Place salmon fillet into the air fryer basket and spread 2 tablespoons of the pesto on each salmon fillet.
5. Sprinkle grated cheese on top of the pesto.
6. Cook salmon for 16 minutes.
7. Serve and enjoy.

Nutritional Value (Amount per Serving):

- Calories 725
- Fat 57 g
- Carbohydrates 4 g
- Sugar 0.7 g
- Protein 49 g
- Cholesterol 108 mg

Spicy Shrimp

Preparation Time: 10 minutes
Cooking Time: 6 minutes
Serve: 2

Ingredients:

- 1/2 lb shrimp, peeled and deveined
- 1/2 tsp old bay seasoning
- 1 tsp cayenne pepper
- 1 tbsp olive oil
- 1/4 tsp paprika
- 1/8 tsp salt

Directions:

1. Preheat the air fryer to 390 F.
2. Add all ingredients into the bowl and toss well.
3. Transfer shrimp into the air fryer basket and cook for 6 minutes.
4. Serve and enjoy.

Nutritional Value (Amount per Serving):

- Calories 195
- Fat 9 g
- Carbohydrates 2 g
- Sugar 0.1 g
- Protein 26 g
- Cholesterol 0 mg

Tilapia Fish Fillets

Preparation Time: 10 minutes
Cooking Time: 7 minutes
Serve: 2

Ingredients:
- 2 tilapia fillets
- 1 tsp old bay seasoning
- 1/2 tsp butter
- 1/4 tsp lemon pepper
- Pepper
- Salt

Directions:
1. Spray air fryer basket with cooking spray.
2. Place fish fillets into the air fryer basket and season with lemon pepper, old bay seasoning, pepper, and salt.
3. Spray fish fillets with cooking spray and cook at 400 F for 7 minutes.
4. Serve and enjoy.

Nutritional Value (Amount per Serving):
- Calories 80
- Fat 2 g
- Carbohydrates 0.2 g
- Sugar 0 g
- Protein 15 g
- Cholesterol 45 mg

Thai Shrimp

Preparation Time: 10 minutes
Cooking Time: 10 minutes
Serve: 4

Ingredients:

- 1 lb shrimp, peeled and deveined
- 1 tsp sesame seeds, toasted
- 2 garlic cloves, minced
- 2 tbsp soy sauce
- 2 tbsp Thai chili sauce
- 1 tbsp arrowroot powder
- 1 tbsp green onion, sliced
- 1/8 tsp ginger, minced

Directions:

1. Spray air fryer basket with cooking spray.
2. Toss shrimp with arrowroot powder and place into the air fryer basket.
3. Cook shrimp at 350 F for 5 minutes. Shake basket well and cook for 5 minutes more.
4. Meanwhile, in a bowl, mix together soy sauce, ginger, garlic, and chili sauce.
5. Add shrimp to the bowl and toss well.
6. Garnish with green onions and sesame seeds.
7. Serve and enjoy.

Nutritional Value (Amount per Serving):

- Calories 155
- Fat 2 g
- Carbohydrates 6 g
- Sugar 2 g
- Protein 25 g
- Cholesterol 0 mg

Miso Fish

Preparation Time: 10 minutes
Cooking Time: 10 minutes
Serve: 2

Ingredients:

- 2 cod fish fillets
- 1 tbsp garlic, chopped
- 2 tsp swerve
- 2 tbsp miso

Directions:

1. Add all ingredients to the zip-lock bag. Shake well place in the refrigerator for overnight.
2. Place marinated fish fillets into the air fryer basket and cook at 350 F for 10 minutes.
3. Serve and enjoy.

Nutritional Value (Amount per Serving):

- Calories 229
- Fat 2.6 g
- Carbohydrates 10.9 g
- Sugar 6.1 g
- Protein 43.4 g
- Cholesterol 99 mg

Tuna Patties

Preparation Time: 10 minutes
Cooking Time: 10 minutes
Serve: 2

Ingredients:

- 2 cans tuna
- 1/2 lemon juice
- 1/2 tsp onion powder
- 1 tsp garlic powder
- 1/2 tsp dried dill
- 1 1/2 tbsp mayonnaise
- 1 1/2 tbsp almond flour
- 1/4 tsp pepper
- 1/4 tsp salt

Directions:

1. Preheat the air fryer to 400 F.
2. Add all ingredients in a mixing bowl and mix until well combined.
3. Spray air fryer basket with cooking spray.
4. Make four patties from mixture and place in the air fryer basket.
5. Cook patties for 10 minutes at 400 F if you want crispier patties then cook for 3 minutes more.
6. Serve and enjoy.

Nutritional Value (Amount per Serving):

- Calories 414
- Fat 20.6 g
- Carbohydrates 5.6 g
- Sugar 1.3 g
- Protein 48.8 g
- Cholesterol 58 mg

Delicious Crab Cakes

Preparation Time: 10 minutes
Cooking Time: 10 minutes
Serve: 4

Ingredients:

- 8 oz crab meat
- 2 tbsp butter, melted
- 2 tsp Dijon mustard
- 1 tbsp mayonnaise
- 1 egg, lightly beaten
- 1/2 tsp old bay seasoning
- 1 green onion, sliced
- 2 tbsp parsley, chopped
- 1/4 cup almond flour
- 1/4 tsp pepper
- 1/2 tsp salt

Directions:

1. Add all ingredients except butter in a mixing bowl and mix until well combined.
2. Make four equal shapes of patties from mixture and place on parchment lined plate.
3. Place plate in the fridge for 30 minutes.
4. Spray air fryer basket with cooking spray.
5. Brush melted butter on both sides of crab patties.
6. Place crab patties in air fryer basket and cook for 10 minutes at 350 F.
7. Turn patties halfway through.
8. Serve and enjoy.

Nutritional Value (Amount per Serving):

- Calories 136
- Fat 12.6 g
- Carbohydrates 4.1 g
- Sugar 0.5 g
- Protein 10.3 g
- Cholesterol 88 mg

Fish Packets

Preparation Time: 10 minutes
Cooking Time: 15 minutes
Serve: 2

Ingredients:

- 2 cod fish fillets
- 1/2 tsp dried tarragon
- 1/2 cup bell peppers, sliced
- 1/4 cup celery, cut into julienne
- 1/2 cup carrots, cut into julienne
- 1 tbsp olive oil
- 1 tbsp lemon juice
- 2 pats butter, melted
- Pepper
- Salt

Directions:

1. In a bowl, mix together butter, lemon juice, tarragon, and salt. Add vegetables and toss well. Set aside.
2. Take two parchments paper pieces to fold vegetables and fish.
3. Spray fish with cooking spray and season with pepper and salt.
4. Place a fish fillet on each parchment paper piece and top with vegetables.
5. Fold parchment paper around the fish and vegetables.
6. Place veggie fish packets into the air fryer basket and cook at 350 F for 15 minutes.
7. Serve and enjoy.

Nutritional Value (Amount per Serving):

- Calories 281
- Fat 8 g
- Carbohydrates 6 g
- Sugar 3 g
- Protein 41 g
- Cholesterol 100 mg

Air Fried King Prawns

Preparation Time: 10 minutes
Cooking Time: 6 minutes
Serve: 4

Ingredients:

- 12 king prawns
- 1 tbsp vinegar
- 1 tbsp ketchup
- 3 tbsp mayonnaise
- 1/2 tsp pepper
- 1 tsp chili powder
- 1 tsp red chili flakes
- 1/2 tsp sea salt

Directions:

1. Preheat the air fryer to 350 F.
2. Spray air fryer basket with cooking spray.
3. Add prawns, chili flakes, chili powder, pepper, and salt to the bowl and toss well.
4. Transfer shrimp to the air fryer basket and cook for 6 minutes.
5. In a small bowl, mix together mayonnaise, ketchup, and vinegar.
6. Serve with mayo mixture and enjoy.

Nutritional Value (Amount per Serving):

- Calories 130
- Fat 5 g
- Carbohydrates 5 g
- Sugar 1 g
- Protein 15 g
- Cholesterol 0 mg

Easy Bacon Shrimp

Preparation Time: 10 minutes
Cooking Time: 7 minutes
Serve: 4

Ingredients:

- 16 shrimp, deveined
- 1/4 tsp pepper
- 16 bacon slices

Directions:

1. Preheat the air fryer to 390 F.
2. Spray air fryer basket with cooking spray.
3. Wrap shrimp with bacon slice and place into the air fryer basket and cook for 5 minutes.
4. Turn shrimp to another side and cook for 2 minutes more. Season shrimp with pepper.
5. Serve and enjoy.

Nutritional Value (Amount per Serving):

- Calories 515
- Fat 33 g
- Carbohydrates 2 g
- Sugar 0 g
- Protein 45 g
- Cholesterol 0 mg

Perfect Salmon Fillets

Preparation Time: 10 minutes
Cooking Time: 15 minutes
Serve: 2

Ingredients:

- 2 salmon fillets
- 1/2 tsp garlic powder
- 1/4 cup plain yogurt
- 1 tsp fresh lemon juice
- 1 tbsp fresh dill, chopped
- 1 lemon, sliced
- Pepper
- Salt

Directions:

1. Place lemon slices into the air fryer basket.
2. Season salmon with pepper and salt and place on top of lemon slices into the air fryer basket.
3. Cook salmon at 330 F for 15 minutes.
4. Meanwhile, in a bowl, mix together yogurt, garlic powder, lemon juice, dill, pepper, and salt.
5. Place salmon on serving plate and top with yogurt mixture.
6. Serve and enjoy.

Nutritional Value (Amount per Serving):

- Calories 195
- Fat 7 g
- Carbohydrates 6 g
- Sugar 2 g
- Protein 24 g
- Cholesterol 65 mg

Lemon Butter Salmon

Preparation Time: 10 minutes
Cooking Time: 11 minutes
Serves 2

Ingredients:

- 2 salmon fillets
- 1/2 tsp olive oil
- 2 tsp garlic, minced
- 2 tbsp butter
- 2 tbsp fresh lemon juice
- 1/4 cup white wine
- Pepper
- Salt

Directions:

1. Preheat the air fryer to 350 F.
2. Spray air fryer basket with cooking spray.
3. Season salmon with pepper and salt and place into the air fryer basket and cook for 6 minutes.
4. Meanwhile, in a saucepan, add remaining ingredients and heat over low heat for 4-5 minutes.
5. Place cooked salmon on serving dish then pour prepared sauce over salmon.
6. Serve and enjoy.

Nutritional Value (Amount per Serving):

- Calories 379
- Fat 23 g
- Carbohydrates 2 g
- Sugar 0.5 g
- Protein 35 g
- Cholesterol 0 mg

Spicy Prawns

Preparation Time: 10 minutes
Cooking Time: 8 minutes
Serve: 2

Ingredients:

- 6 prawns
- 1/4 tsp pepper
- 1/2 tsp chili powder
- 1 tsp chili flakes
- 1/4 tsp salt

Directions:

1. Preheat the air fryer to 350 F.
2. In a bowl, mix together spices add prawns.
3. Spray air fryer basket with cooking spray.
4. Transfer prawns into the air fryer basket and cook for 8 minutes.
5. Serve and enjoy.

Nutritional Value (Amount per Serving):

- Calories 80
- Fat 1.2 g
- Carbohydrates 1 g
- Sugar 0.1 g
- Protein 15.2 g
- Cholesterol 140 mg

Simple Salmon Patties

Preparation Time: 10 minutes
Cooking Time: 10 minutes
Serve: 2

Ingredients:

- 14 oz salmon
- 1/2 onion, diced
- 1 egg, lightly beaten
- 1 tsp dill
- 1/2 cup almond flour

Directions:

1. Spray air fryer basket with cooking spray.
2. Add all ingredients into the bowl and mix until well combined.
3. Spray air fryer basket with cooking spray.
4. Make patties from salmon mixture and place into the air fryer basket.
5. Cook at 370 F for 5 minutes.
6. Turn patties to another side and cook for 5 minutes more.
7. Serve and enjoy.

Nutritional Value (Amount per Serving):

- Calories 350
- Fat 15 g
- Carbohydrates 3 g
- Sugar 1 g
- Protein 44 g
- Cholesterol 0 mg

Creamy Shrimp

Preparation Time: 10 minutes
Cooking Time: 8 minutes
Serve: 4

Ingredients:

- 1 lb shrimp, peeled
- 1 tbsp garlic, minced
- 1 tbsp tomato ketchup
- 3 tbsp mayonnaise
- 1/2 tsp paprika
- 1 tsp sriracha
- 1/2 tsp salt

Directions:

1. In a bowl, mix together mayonnaise, paprika, sriracha, garlic, ketchup, and salt. Add shrimp and stir well.
2. Add shrimp mixture into the air fryer baking dish and place in the air fryer.
3. Cook at 325 F for 8 minutes. Stir halfway through.
4. Serve and enjoy.

Nutritional Value (Amount per Serving):

- Calories 185
- Fat 5 g
- Carbohydrates 6 g
- Sugar 1 g
- Protein 25 g
- Cholesterol 0 mg

Lemon Crab Patties

Preparation Time: 10 minutes
Cooking Time: 10 minutes
Serve: 4

Ingredients:

- 1 egg
- 12 oz crabmeat
- 2 green onion, chopped
- 1/4 cup mayonnaise
- 1 cup almond flour
- 1 tsp old bay seasoning
- 1 tsp red pepper flakes
- 1 tbsp fresh lemon juice

Directions:

1. Preheat the air fryer to 400 F.
2. Spray air fryer basket with cooking spray.
3. Add 1/2 almond flour into the mixing bowl.
4. Add remaining ingredients and mix until well combined.
5. Make patties from mixture and coat with remaining almond flour and place into the air fryer basket.
6. Cook patties for 5 minutes then turn to another side and cook for 5 minutes more.
7. Serve and enjoy.

Nutritional Value (Amount per Serving):

- Calories 184
- Fat 11 g
- Carbohydrates 5 g
- Sugar 1 g
- Protein 12 g
- Cholesterol 0 mg

Cheesy Crab Dip

Preparation Time: 10 minutes
Cooking Time: 7 minutes
Serve: 4

Ingredients:

- 1 cup crabmeat, cooked
- 2 tbsp fresh parsley, chopped
- 2 tbsp fresh lemon juice
- 2 cups Jalapeno jack cheese, grated
- 2 tbsp hot sauce
- 1/2 cup green onions, sliced
- 1/4 cup mayonnaise
- 1 tsp pepper
- 1/2 tsp salt

Directions:

1. Add all ingredients except parsley and lemon juice in air fryer baking dish and stir well.
2. Place dish in the air fryer basket and cook at 400 F for 7 minutes.
3. Add parsley and lemon juice. Mix well.
4. Serve and enjoy.

Nutritional Value (Amount per Serving):

- Calories 305
- Fat 22 g
- Carbohydrates 5 g
- Sugar 1 g
- Protein 20 g
- Cholesterol 0 mg

Chili Garlic Shrimp

Preparation Time: 10 minutes
Cooking Time: 7 minutes
Serves 4

Ingredients:

- 1 lb shrimp, peeled and deveined
- 1 tbsp olive oil
- 1 lemon, sliced
- 1 red chili pepper, sliced
- 1/2 tsp garlic powder
- Pepper
- Salt

Directions:

1. Preheat the air fryer to 400 F.
2. Spray air fryer basket with cooking spray.
3. Add all ingredients into the bowl and toss well.
4. Add shrimp into the air fryer basket and cook for 5 minutes. Shake basket twice.
5. Serve and enjoy.

Nutritional Value (Amount per Serving):

- Calories 170
- Fat 5 g
- Carbohydrates 3 g
- Sugar 0.5 g
- Protein 25 g
- Cholesterol 0 mg

Chapter 8: Meatless Meals Recipes

Quick Creamy Spinach

Preparation Time: 10 minutes
Cooking Time: 15 minutes
Serve: 2

Ingredients:

- 10 oz frozen spinach, thawed
- 1/4 cup parmesan cheese, shredded
- 1/2 tsp ground nutmeg
- 1 tsp pepper
- 4 oz cream cheese, diced
- 2 tsp garlic, minced
- 1 small onion, chopped
- 1 tsp salt

Directions:

1. Spray 6-inch pan with cooking spray and set aside.
2. In a bowl, mix together spinach, cream cheese, garlic, onion, nutmeg, pepper, and salt.
3. Pour spinach mixture into the prepared pan.
4. Place dish in air fryer basket and air fry at 350 F for 10 minutes.
5. Open air fryer basket and sprinkle parmesan cheese on top of spinach mixture and air fry at 400 F for 5 minutes more.
6. Serve and enjoy.

Nutritional Value (Amount per Serving):

- Calories 265
- Fat 21.4 g
- Carbohydrates 11.9 g
- Sugar 2.4 g
- Protein 10.2 g
- Cholesterol 65 mg

Cauliflower Rice

Preparation Time: 10 minutes
Cooking Time: 12 minutes
Serves 3

Ingredients:

- 1 cauliflower head, cut into florets
- 2 tbsp olive oil
- 2 garlic cloves, chopped
- 1 tomato, chopped
- 1 onion, chopped
- 2 tbsp tomato paste
- 1 tsp white pepper
- 1 tsp pepper
- 1 tbsp dried thyme
- 2 chilies, chopped
- 1/2 tsp salt

Directions:

1. Preheat the air fryer to 370 F.
2. Add cauliflower florets into the food processor and process until it looks like rice.
3. Stir in tomato paste, tomatoes, and spices and mix well.
4. Add cauliflower mixture into the air fryer baking pan and drizzle with olive oil.
5. Place pan in the air fryer and cook for 12 minutes.
6. Serve and enjoy.

Nutritional Value (Amount per Serving):

- Calories 135
- Fat 9.7 g
- Carbohydrates 13 g
- Sugar 4 g
- Protein 3.2 g
- Cholesterol 0 mg

Curried Eggplant Slices

Preparation Time: 10 minutes
Cooking Time: 10 minutes
Serve: 2

Ingredients:

- 1 large eggplant, cut into 1/2-inch thick slices
- 1 garlic clove, minced
- 1 tbsp olive oil
- 1/2 tsp curry powder
- 1/8 tsp turmeric
- Salt

Directions:

1. Preheat the air fryer to 300 F.
2. Add all ingredients into the large mixing bowl and toss to coat.
3. Transfer eggplant slices into the air fryer basket.
4. Cook eggplant slices for 10 minutes or until lightly brown. Shake basket halfway through.
5. Serve and enjoy.

Nutritional Value (Amount per Serving):

- Calories 122
- Fat 7.5 g
- Carbohydrates 14.4 g
- Sugar 6.9 g
- Protein 2.4 g
- Cholesterol 0 mg

Tasty Okra

Preparation Time: 10 minutes
Cooking Time: 12 minutes
Serve: 2

Ingredients:

- 1/2 lb okra, ends trimmed and sliced
- 1 tsp olive oil
- 1/2 tsp mango powder
- 1/2 tsp chili powder
- 1/2 tsp ground coriander
- 1/2 tsp ground cumin
- 1/8 tsp pepper
- 1/4 tsp salt

Directions:

1. Preheat the air fryer to 350 F.
2. Add all ingredients into the large bowl and toss well.
3. Spray air fryer basket with cooking spray.
4. Transfer okra mixture into the air fryer basket and cook for 10 minutes. Shake basket halfway through.
5. Toss okra well and cook for 2 minutes more.
6. Serve and enjoy.

Nutritional Value (Amount per Serving):

- Calories 70
- Fat 2.8 g
- Carbohydrates 9.1 g
- Sugar 1.7 g
- Protein 2.4 g
- Cholesterol 0 mg

Air Fried Onion & Bell Peppers

Preparation Time: 10 minutes
Cooking Time: 25 minutes
Serve: 3

Ingredients:

- 6 bell pepper, sliced
- 1 tbsp Italian seasoning
- 1 tbsp olive oil
- 1 onion, sliced

Directions:

1. Add all ingredients into the large mixing bowl and toss well.
2. Preheat the air fryer to 320 F.
3. Transfer bell pepper and onion mixture into the air fryer basket and cook for 15 minutes.
4. Toss well and cook for 10 minutes more.
5. Serve and enjoy.

Nutritional Value (Amount per Serving):

- Calories 129
- Fat 6.1g
- Carbohydrates 14 g
- Sugar 10 g
- Protein 3 g
- Cholesterol 3 mg

Tasty Herb Tomatoes

Preparation Time: 10 minutes
Cooking Time: 15 minutes
Serve. 1

Ingredients:

- 2 large tomatoes, halved
- 1 tbsp olive oil
- 1/2 tsp thyme, chopped
- 2 garlic cloves, minced
- Pepper
- Salt

Directions:

1. Add all ingredients into the bowl and toss well.
2. Transfer tomatoes into the air fryer basket and cook at 390 F for 15 minutes.
3. Serve and enjoy.

Nutritional Value (Amount per Serving):

- Calories 49
- Fat 3.7 g
- Carbohydrates 4.1 g
- Sugar 2.4 g
- Protein 0.9 g
- Cholesterol 0 mg

Asian Broccoli

Preparation Time: 10 minutes
Cooking Time: 20 minutes
Serve: 4

Ingredients:

- 1 lb broccoli, cut into florets
- 1 tsp rice vinegar
- 2 tsp sriracha
- 2 tbsp soy sauce
- 1 tbsp garlic, minced
- 5 drops liquid stevia
- 1 1/2 tbsp sesame oil
- Salt

Directions:

1. In a bowl, toss together broccoli, garlic, oil, and salt.
2. Spread broccoli in air fryer basket and cook for 15-20 minutes at 400 F.
3. Meanwhile, in a microwave-safe bowl mix together soy sauce, vinegar, liquid stevia, and sriracha and microwave for 10 seconds.
4. Transfer broccoli to a bowl and toss well with soy mixture to coat.
5. Serve and enjoy.

Nutritional Value (Amount per Serving):

- Calories 94
- Fat 5.5 g
- Carbohydrates 9.3 g
- Sugar 2.1 g
- Protein 3.8 g
- Cholesterol 0 mg

Crisp & Tender Brussels sprouts

Preparation Time: 10 minutes
Cooking Time: 10 minutes
Serve: 2

Ingredients:

- 2 cups Brussels sprouts, sliced
- 1 tbsp balsamic vinegar
- 1 tbsp olive oil
- 1/4 tsp sea salt

Directions:

1. Add all ingredients into the large bowl and toss well.
2. Spray air fryer basket with cooking spray.
3. Transfer Brussels sprouts mixture into the air fryer basket.
4. Cook Brussels sprouts at 400 F for 10 minutes. Shake basket halfway through.
5. Serve and enjoy.

Nutritional Value (Amount per Serving):

- Calories 100
- Fat 7.3 g
- Carbohydrates 8.1 g
- Sugar 1.9 g
- Protein 3 g
- Cholesterol 0 mg

Curried Sweet Potato Fries

Preparation Time: 10 minutes
Cooking Time: 20 minutes
Serve: 3

Ingredients:

- 2 sweet potatoes, peeled and cut into fries shape
- 1/4 tsp ground coriander
- 1/2 tsp curry powder
- 2 tbsp olive oil
- Pepper
- Salt

Directions:

1. Add all ingredients into the mixing bowl and toss to coat.
2. Transfer sweet potato fries into the air fryer basket and cook at 370 F for 20 minutes. Toss halfway through.
3. Serve and enjoy.

Nutritional Value (Amount per Serving):

- Calories 118
- Fat 9 g
- Carbohydrates 9 g
- Sugar 2 g
- Protein 1 g
- Cholesterol 0 mg

Mushroom Bean Casserole

Preparation Time: 10 minutes
Cooking Time: 12 minutes
Serve: 6

Ingredients:

- 2 cups mushrooms, sliced
- 1 tsp onion powder
- 1/2 tsp ground sage
- 1/2 tbsp garlic powder
- 1 fresh lemon juice
- 1 1/2 lbs green beans, trimmed
- 1/4 tsp pepper
- 1/2 tsp salt

Directions:

1. In a large mixing bowl, toss together green beans, onion powder, sage, garlic powder, lemon juice, mushrooms, pepper, and salt.
2. Spray air fryer basket with cooking spray.
3. Transfer green bean mixture into the air fryer basket.
4. Cook for 10-12 minutes at 400 F. Shake after every 3 minutes.
5. Serve and enjoy.

Nutritional Value (Amount per Serving):

- Calories 45
- Fat 0.2 g
- Carbohydrates 9.8 g
- Sugar 2.3g
- Protein 3 g
- Cholesterol 0 mg

Crispy Pickles

Preparation Time: 10 minutes
Cooking Time: 6 minutes
Serve: 4

Ingredients:

- 16 dill pickles, sliced
- 1 egg, lightly beaten
- 1/2 cup almond flour
- 3 tbsp parmesan cheese, grated
- 1/2 cup pork rind, crushed

Directions:

1. Take three bowls. Mix together pork rinds and cheese in the first bowl.
2. In a second bowl, add the egg.
3. In the last bowl add the almond flour.
4. Coat each pickle slice with almond flour then dip in egg and finally coat with pork and cheese mixture.
5. Spray air fryer basket with cooking spray.
6. Place coated pickles in the air fryer basket.
7. Cook pickles for 6 minutes at 370 F.
8. Serve and enjoy.

Nutritional Value (Amount per Serving):

- Calories 245
- Fat 17 g
- Carbohydrates 4 g
- Sugar 2 g
- Protein 17 g
- Cholesterol 41 mg

Spiced Green Beans

Preparation Time: 10 minutes
Cooking Time: 10 minutes
Serve: 2

Ingredients:

- 2 cups green beans
- 1/8 tsp cayenne pepper
- 1/8 tsp ground allspice
- 1/4 tsp ground cinnamon
- 1/2 tsp dried oregano
- 2 tbsp olive oil
- 1/4 tsp ground coriander
- 1/4 tsp ground cumin
- 1/2 tsp salt

Directions:

1. Add all ingredients into the large bowl and toss well.
2. Spray air fryer basket with cooking spray.
3. Add bowl mixture into the air fryer basket.
4. Cook at 370 F for 10 minutes. Shake basket halfway through
5. Serve and enjoy.

Nutritional Value (Amount per Serving):

- Calories 155
- Fat 14 g
- Carbohydrates 8 g
- Sugar 1 g
- Protein 2 g
- Cholesterol 0 mg

Squash Fritters

Preparation Time: 10 minutes
Cooking Time: 7 minutes
Serve: 4

Ingredients:

- 1 yellow summer squash, grated
- 1 egg, lightly beaten
- 3 oz cream cheese
- 2 tbsp olive oil
- 1/2 tsp dried oregano
- 1/4 cup almond flour
- 1/3 cup carrot, grated
- Pepper
- Salt

Directions:

1. Spray air fryer basket with cooking spray.
2. Add all ingredients into the mixing bowl and mix until well combined.
3. Make patties from bowl mixture and place into the air fryer basket and cook at 400 F for 7 minutes.
4. Serve and enjoy.

Nutritional Value (Amount per Serving):

- Calories 190
- Fat 18.6 g
- Carbohydrates 2.9 g
- Sugar 0.8 g
- Protein 4.4 g
- Cholesterol 64 mg

Roasted Carrots

Preparation Time: 10 minutes
Cooking Time: 25 minutes
Serve: 6

Ingredients:

- 16 small carrots
- 1 tbsp fresh parsley, chopped
- 1 tbsp dried basil
- 6 garlic cloves, minced
- 4 tbsp olive oil
- 1 1/2 tsp salt

Directions:

1. Preheat the air fryer to 350 F.
2. In a bowl, mix together oil, carrots, basil, garlic, and salt.
3. Transfer carrots into the air fryer basket and cook for 20-25 minutes. Shake basket 2-3 times while cooking.
4. Garnish with parsley and serve.

Nutritional Value (Amount per Serving):

- Calories 140
- Fat 9.4 g
- Carbohydrates 14 g
- Sugar 5 g
- Protein 1.3 g
- Cholesterol 0 mg

Ratatouille

Preparation Time: 10 minutes
Cooking Time: 25 minutes
Serve: 4

Ingredients:

- 1 tomato, cubed
- 1 zucchini, cubed
- 1/2 small eggplant, cubed
- 1 garlic clove, crushed
- 2 oregano sprigs, chopped
- 1 cayenne pepper, cubed
- 1/2 onion, cubed
- 1 bell pepper, cubed
- 1 tbsp vinegar
- 1 tbsp white wine
- 1 tbsp olive oil
- Pepper
- Salt

Directions:

1. Add all ingredients into the large mixing bowl and toss well.
2. Transfer vegetable mixture into the air fryer baking dish and place in the air fryer.
3. Cook at 400 F for 25 minutes. Stir after every 5 minutes.
4. Serve and enjoy.

Nutritional Value (Amount per Serving):

- Calories 79
- Fat 4 g
- Carbohydrates 10.3 g
- Sugar 5.2 g
- Protein 1.9 g
- Cholesterol 0 mg

Zucchini Fries

Preparation Time: 10 minutes
Cooking Time: 15 minutes
Serve: 2

Ingredients:

- 2 medium zucchini, cut into French fries shape
- 2 tbsp arrowroot powder
- 1 tbsp water
- 1/2 tbsp olive oil
- Salt

Directions

1. Preheat the air fryer to 390 F.
2. Add all ingredients into the bowl and mix well.
3. Place coated zucchini fries in air fryer basket and air fry for 15 minutes.
4. Serve and enjoy.

Nutritional Value (Amount per Serving):

- Calories 90
- Fat 4 g
- Carbohydrates 13 g
- Sugar 3.4 g
- Protein 2.4 g
- Cholesterol 0 mg

Simple Taro Fries

Preparation Time: 10 minutes
Cooking Time: 20 minutes
Serve: 2

Ingredients:

- 8 small taro, peel and cut into fries shape
- 1 tbsp olive oil
- 1/2 tsp salt

Directions:

1. Add taro slice in a bowl and toss well with olive oil and salt.
2. Transfer taro slices into the air fryer basket.
3. Cook at 360 F for 20 minutes. Toss halfway through.
4. Serve and enjoy.

Nutritional Value (Amount per Serving):

- Calories 115
- Fat 7 g
- Carbohydrates 12 g
- Sugar 0.2 g
- Protein 0.8 g
- Cholesterol 0 mg

Spicy Buffalo Cauliflower

Preparation Time: 10 minutes
Cooking Time: 15 minutes
Serve: 4

Ingredients:

- 8 oz cauliflower florets
- 1 tsp cayenne pepper
- 1 tsp chili powder
- 1 tsp olive oil
- 1 tsp garlic, minced
- 1 tomato, diced
- 6 tbsp almond flour
- 1 tsp black pepper
- 1/2 tsp salt

Directions:

1. Preheat the air fryer to 350 F.
2. Spray air fryer basket with cooking spray.
3. Add tomato, garlic, black pepper, olive oil, cayenne pepper, and chili powder into the blender and blend until smooth.
4. Add cauliflower florets into the bowl. Season with pepper and salt.
5. Pour blended mixture over cauliflower florets and toss well to coat.
6. Coat cauliflower florets with almond flour and place into the air fryer basket and cook for 15 minutes. Shake basket 2-3 times.
7. Serve and enjoy.

Nutritional Value (Amount per Serving):

- Calories 92
- Fat 6 g
- Carbohydrates 7 g
- Sugar 2 g
- Protein 3 g
- Cholesterol 0 mg

Ricotta Mushrooms

Preparation Time: 10 minutes
Cooking Time: 12 minutes
Serve: 4

Ingredients:
- 4 large Portobello mushrooms caps
- 1 tbsp olive oil
- 1/4 cup parmesan cheese, grated
- 1/4 tsp rosemary, chopped
- 1 cup spinach, chopped
- 1/4 cup ricotta cheese

Directions:
1. Coat mushrooms with olive oil.
2. Transfer mushrooms into the air fryer basket and cook at 350 F for 2 minutes.
3. In a bowl, mix together remaining ingredients.
4. Stuff bowl mixture into the mushrooms and place into the air fryer basket and cook for 10 minutes more.
5. Serve and enjoy.

Nutritional Value (Amount per Serving):
- Calories 69
- Fat 5.1 g
- Carbohydrates 2.2 g
- Sugar 0.1 g
- Protein 3.5 g
- Cholesterol 6 mg

Parmesan Broccoli

Preparation Time: 10 minutes
Cooking Time: 5 minutes
Serve: 2

Ingredients:

- 3 cups broccoli florets
- 1/4 cup parmesan cheese, grated
- 2 tbsp olive oil
- 2 garlic cloves, minced

Directions:

1. Preheat the air fryer to 360 F.
2. Add all ingredients into the large bowl and toss well.
3. Transfer broccoli mixture into the air fryer basket and cook for 4-5 minutes.
4. Serve and enjoy.

Nutritional Value (Amount per Serving):

- Calories 182
- Fat 15.2 g
- Carbohydrates 10.2 g
- Sugar 2.4 g
- Protein 5.1 g
- Cholesterol 3 mg

Chapter 9: Desserts Recipes

Egg Custard

Preparation Time: 10 minutes
Cooking Time: 32 minutes
Serve: 6
Ingredients:
- 2 egg yolks
- 3 eggs
- 1/2 cup erythritol
- 2 cups heavy whipping cream
- 1/2 tsp vanilla
- 1 tsp nutmeg

Directions:
1. Preheat the air fryer to 325 F.
2. Add all ingredients into the large bowl and beat until well combined.
3. Pour custard mixture into the greased baking dish and place into the air fryer.
4. Cook for 32 minutes.
5. Let it cool completely then place in the refrigerator for 1-2 hours.
6. Serve and enjoy.

Nutritional Value (Amount per Serving):
- Calories 190
- Fat 19 g
- Carbohydrates 2 g
- Sugar 0.5 g
- Protein 5 g
- Cholesterol 26 mg

Pecan Muffins

Preparation Time: 10 minutes
Cooking Time: 15 minutes
Serve: 12

Ingredients:

- 4 eggs
- 1 tsp vanilla
- 1/4 cup almond milk
- 2 tbsp butter, melted
- 1/2 cup swerve
- 1 tsp psyllium husk
- 1 tbsp baking powder
- 1/2 cup pecans, chopped
- 1/2 tsp ground cinnamon
- 2 tsp allspice
- 1 1/2 cups almond flour

Directions:

1. Preheat the air fryer to 370 F.
2. Beat eggs, almond milk, vanilla, sweetener, and butter in a bowl using a hand mixer until smooth.
3. Add remaining ingredients and mix until well combined.
4. Pour batter into the silicone muffin molds and place into the air fryer basket in batches.
5. Cook muffins for 15 minutes.
6. Serve and enjoy.

Nutritional Value (Amount per Serving):

- Calories 204
- Fat 18 g
- Carbohydrates 6 g
- Sugar 1.2 g
- Protein 5 g
- Cholesterol 60 mg

Chocolate Brownie

Preparation Time: 10 minutes
Cooking Time: 16 minutes
Serve: 4

Ingredients:

- 1 cup bananas, overripe
- 1 scoop protein powder
- 2 tbsp unsweetened cocoa powder
- 1/2 cup almond butter, melted

Directions:

1. Preheat the air fryer to 325 F.
2. Spray air fryer baking pan with cooking spray.
3. Add all ingredients into the blender and blend until smooth.
4. Pour batter into the prepared pan and place in the air fryer basket.
5. Cook brownie for 16 minutes.
6. Serve and enjoy.

Nutritional Value (Amount per Serving):

- Calories 80
- Fat 2.1 g
- Carbohydrates 11.4 g
- Protein 7 g
- Sugars 5 g
- Cholesterol 15 mg

Easy Lava Cake

Preparation Time: 10 minutes
Cooking Time: 9 minutes
Serve: 2

Ingredients:

- 1 egg
- 1/2 tsp baking powder
- 1 tbsp coconut oil, melted
- 1 tbsp flax meal
- 2 tbsp erythritol
- 2 tbsp water
- 2 tbsp unsweetened cocoa powder
- Pinch of salt

Directions:

1. Whisk all ingredients into the bowl and transfer in two ramekins.
2. Preheat the air fryer to 350 F.
3. Place ramekins in air fryer basket and bake for 8-9 minutes.
4. Carefully remove ramekins from air fryer and let it cool for 10 minutes.
5. Serve and enjoy.

Nutritional Value (Amount per Serving):

- Calories 119
- Fat 11 g
- Carbohydrates 4 g
- Sugar 0.3 g
- Protein 5 g
- Cholesterol 82 mg

Apple Chips with Dip

Preparation Time: 10 minutes
Cooking Time: 12 minutes
Serve: 4

Ingredients:

- 1 apple, thinly slice using a mandolin slicer
- 1 tbsp almond butter
- 1/4 cup plain yogurt
- 2 tsp olive oil
- 1 tsp ground cinnamon
- 4 drops liquid stevia

Directions:

1. Add apple slices, oil, and cinnamon in a large bowl and toss well.
2. Spray air fryer basket with cooking spray.
3. Place apple slices in air fryer basket and cook at 375 F for 12 minutes. Turn after every 4 minutes.
4. Meanwhile, in a small bowl, mix together almond butter, yogurt, and sweetener.
5. Serve apple chips with dip and enjoy.

Nutritional Value (Amount per Serving):

- Calories 86
- Fat 4.9 g
- Carbohydrates 10 g
- Sugar 7.1 g
- Protein 1.9 g
- Cholesterol 1 mg

Delicious Spiced Apples

Preparation Time: 10 minutes
Cooking Time: 10 minutes
Serve: 6

Ingredients:

- 4 small apples, sliced
- 1 tsp apple pie spice
- 1/2 cup erythritol
- 2 tbsp coconut oil, melted

Directions:

1. Add apple slices in a mixing bowl and sprinkle sweetener, apple pie spice, and coconut oil over apple and toss to coat.
2. Transfer apple slices in air fryer dish. Place dish in air fryer basket and cook at 350 F for 10 minutes.
3. Serve and enjoy.

Nutritional Value (Amount per Serving):

- Calories 73
- Fat 4.6 g
- Carbohydrates 8.2 g
- Sugar 5.4 g
- Protein 0 g
- Cholesterol 0 mg

Tasty Cheese Bites

Preparation Time: 10 minutes
Cooking Time: 2 minutes
Serve: 16

Ingredients:
- 8 oz cream cheese, softened
- 2 tbsp erythritol
- 1/2 cup almond flour
- 1/2 tsp vanilla
- 4 tbsp heavy cream
- 1/2 cup erythritol

Directions:
1. Add cream cheese, vanilla, 1/2 cup erythritol, and 2 tbsp heavy cream in a stand mixer and mix until smooth.
2. Scoop cream cheese mixture onto the parchment lined plate and place in the refrigerator for 1 hour.
3. In a small bowl, mix together almond flour and 2 tbsp erythritol.
4. Dip cheesecake bites in remaining heavy cream and coat with almond flour mixture.
5. Place prepared cheesecake bites in air fryer basket and air fry for 2 minutes at 350 F.
6. Make sure cheesecake bites are frozen before air fry otherwise they will melt.
7. Drizzle with chocolate syrup and serve.

Nutritional Value (Amount per Serving):
- Calories 80
- Fat 7 g
- Carbohydrates 2 g
- Sugar 1 g
- Protein 2 g
- Cholesterol 16 mg

Blueberry Muffins

Preparation Time: 10 minutes
Cooking Time: 20 minutes
Serve: 12

Ingredients:

- 3 large eggs
- 1/3 cup coconut oil, melted
- 1 1/2 tsp gluten-free baking powder
- 1/2 cup erythritol
- 2 1/2 cups almond flour
- 3/4 cup blueberries
- 1/2 tsp vanilla
- 1/3 cup unsweetened almond milk

Directions:

1. Preheat the air fryer to 325 F.
2. In a large bowl, stir together almond flour, baking powder, erythritol.
3. Mix in the coconut oil, vanilla, eggs, and almond milk. Add blueberries and fold well.
4. Pour batter into the silicone muffin molds and place into the air fryer basket in batches.
5. Cook muffins for 20 minutes.
6. Serve and enjoy.

Nutritional Value (Amount per Serving):

- Calories 215
- Fat 19 g
- Carbohydrates 5 g
- Sugar 2 g
- Protein 7 g
- Cholesterol 45 mg

Cappuccino Muffins

Preparation Time: 10 minutes
Cooking Time: 20 minutes
Serve: 12

Ingredients:

- 4 eggs
- 2 cups almond flour
- 1/2 tsp vanilla
- 1 tsp espresso powder
- 1/2 cup sour cream
- 1 tsp cinnamon
- 2 tsp baking powder
- 1/4 cup coconut flour
- 1/2 cup Swerve
- 1/4 tsp salt

Directions:

1. Preheat the air fryer to 325 F.
2. Add sour cream, vanilla, espresso powder, and eggs in a blender and blend until smooth.
3. Add almond flour, cinnamon, baking powder, coconut flour, sweetener, and salt. Blend again until smooth.
4. Pour batter into the silicone muffin molds and place into the air fryer basket. (Cook in batches)
5. Cook muffins for 20 minutes.
6. Serve and enjoy.

Nutritional Value (Amount per Serving):

- Calories 150
- Fat 13 g
- Carbohydrates 5.3 g
- Sugar 0.8 g
- Protein 6 g
- Cholesterol 59 mg

Pumpkin Cookies

Preparation Time: 10 minutes
Cooking Time: 20 minutes
Serve: 27

Ingredients:

- 1 egg
- 2 cups almond flour
- 1/2 tsp baking powder
- 1 tsp vanilla
- 1/2 cup butter
- 15 drops liquid stevia
- 1/2 tsp pumpkin pie spice
- 1/2 cup pumpkin puree

Directions:

1. Preheat the air fryer to 280 F.
2. In a large bowl, add all ingredients and mix until well combined.
3. Make cookies from mixture and place into the air fryer and cook for 20 minutes.
4. Serve and enjoy.

Nutritional Value (Amount per Serving):

- Calories 80
- Fat 7 g
- Carbohydrates 2 g
- Sugar 1 g
- Protein 3 g
- Cholesterol 25 mg

Crustless Pie

Preparation Time: 10 minutes
Cooking Time: 24 minutes
Serve: 4

Ingredients:

- 3 eggs
- 1/2 cup pumpkin puree
- 1/2 tsp cinnamon
- 1 tsp vanilla
- 1/4 cup erythritol
- 1/2 cup cream
- 1/2 cup unsweetened almond milk

Directions:

1. Preheat the air fryer to 325 F.
2. Spray air fryer baking dish with cooking spray and set aside.
3. In a large bowl, add all ingredients and beat until smooth.
4. Pour pie mixture into the prepared dish and place into the air fryer and cook for 24 minutes.
5. Let it cool completely and place into the refrigerator for 1-2 hours.
6. Slice and serve.

Nutritional Value (Amount per Serving):

- Calories 85
- Fat 5 g
- Carbohydrates 4 g
- Sugar 1 g
- Protein 5 g
- Cholesterol 35 mg

Cinnamon Apple Chips

Preparation Time: 10 minutes
Cooking Time: 8 minutes
Serve: 6

Ingredients:
- 3 Granny Smith apples, wash, core and thinly slice
- 1 tsp ground cinnamon
- Pinch of salt

Directions:
1. Rub apple slices with cinnamon and salt and place into the air fryer basket.
2. Cook at 390 F for 8 minutes. Turn halfway through.
3. Serve and enjoy.

Nutritional Value (Amount per Serving):
- Calories 41
- Fat 0 g
- Carbohydrates 11 g
- Sugar 8 g
- Protein 0 g
- Cholesterol 0 mg

Almond Coconut Lemon Cake

Preparation Time: 10 minutes
Cooking Time: 48 minutes
Serve: 10

Ingredients:

- 4 eggs
- 2 tbsp lemon zest
- 1/2 cup butter softened
- 2 tsp baking powder
- 1/4 cup coconut flour
- 2 cups almond flour
- 1/2 cup fresh lemon juice
- 1/4 cup swerve
- 1 tbsp vanilla

Directions:

1. Preheat the air fryer to 280 F.
2. Spray air fryer baking dish with cooking spray and set aside.
3. In a large bowl, beat all ingredients using a hand mixer until a smooth.
4. Pour batter into the prepared dish and place into the air fryer and cook for 48 minutes.
5. Slice and serve.

Nutritional Value (Amount per Serving):

- Calories 245
- Fat 22 g
- Carbohydrates 5 g
- Sugar 2 g
- Protein 7 g
- Cholesterol 24 mg

Vanilla Coconut Cheese Cookies

Preparation Time: 10 minutes
Cooking Time: 12 minutes
Serve: 15

Ingredients:

- 1 egg
- 1/2 tsp baking powder
- 1 tsp vanilla
- 1/2 cup swerve
- 1/2 cup butter, softened
- 3 tbsp cream cheese, softened
- 1/2 cup coconut flour
- Pinch of salt

Directions:

1. In a bowl, beat together butter, sweetener, and cream cheese.
2. Add egg and vanilla and beat until smooth and creamy.
3. Add coconut flour, salt, and baking powder and beat until combined. Cover and place in the fridge for 1 hour.
4. Preheat the air fryer to 325 F.
5. Make cookies from dough and place into the air fryer and cook for 12 minutes.
6. Serve and enjoy.

Nutritional Value (Amount per Serving):

- Calories 65
- Fat 7 g
- Carbohydrates 1 g
- Sugar 0.5 g
- Protein 1 g
- Cholesterol 34 mg

Chocolate Custard

Preparation Time: 10 minutes
Cooking Time: 32 minutes
Serve: 4

Ingredients:

- 2 eggs
- 1 tsp vanilla
- 1 cup heavy whipping cream
- 1 cup unsweetened almond milk
- 2 tbsp unsweetened cocoa powder
- 1/4 cup Swerve
- Pinch of salt

Directions:

1. Preheat the air fryer to 305 F.
2. Add all ingredients into the blender and blend until well combined.
3. Pour mixture into the ramekins and place into the air fryer.
4. Cook for 32 minutes.
5. Serve and enjoy.

Nutritional Value (Amount per Serving):

- Calories 156
- Fat 15 g
- Carbohydrates 3 g
- Sugar 0.5 g
- Protein 4 g
- Cholesterol 35 mg

Chia Chocolate Cookies

Preparation Time: 5 minutes
Cooking Time: 8 minutes
Serve: 20

Ingredients:

- 2 1/2 tbsp ground chia
- 2 tbsp chocolate protein powder
- 1 cup sunflower seed butter
- 1 cup almond flour

Directions:

1. Preheat the air fryer to 325 F.
2. In a large bowl, add all ingredients and mix until combined.
3. Make cookies from bowl mixture and place into the air fryer and cook for 8 minutes.
4. Serve and enjoy.

Nutritional Value (Amount per Serving):

- Calories 110
- Fat 9 g
- Carbohydrates 5 g
- Sugar 0.5 g
- Protein 4 g
- Cholesterol 35 mg

Cinnamon Pecan Muffins

Preparation Time: 10 minutes
Cooking Time: 15 minutes
Serve: 12

Ingredients:

- 4 eggs
- 1 1/2 cups almond flour
- 1 tsp vanilla
- 1/4 cup unsweetened almond milk
- 2 tbsp butter, melted
- 1/2 cup erythritol
- 1 tsp psyllium husk
- 1/2 cup pecans, chopped
- 1/2 tsp ground cinnamon
- 2 tsp allspice
- 1 tbsp baking powder

Directions:

1. Preheat the air fryer to 400 F.
2. Beat eggs, milk, vanilla, sweetener, and butter in a bowl using a hand mixer until smooth.
3. Add remaining ingredients and stir until combined.
4. Pour batter into silicone muffin molds and place in the air fryer. In batches.
5. Cook for 15 minutes.
6. Serve and enjoy.

Nutritional Value (Amount per Serving):

- Calories 95
- Fat 8 g
- Carbohydrates 3 g
- Sugar 0.5 g
- Protein 3 g
- Cholesterol 28 mg

Cheese Butter Cookies

Preparation Time: 10 minutes
Cooking Time: 12 minutes
Serve: 8

Ingredients:

- 2 eggs
- 5 tbsp butter, melted
- 1/3 cup sour cream
- 1/3 cup mozzarella cheese, shredded
- 1 1/4 cup almond flour
- 1/2 tsp baking powder
- 1/2 tsp salt

Directions:

1. Preheat the air fryer to 370 F.
2. Add all ingredients into a large bowl and mix using a hand mixer.
3. Spoon batter into the mini silicone muffin molds and place into the air fryer and cook for 12 minutes.
4. Serve and enjoy.

Nutritional Value (Amount per Serving):

- Calories 205
- Fat 20 g
- Carbohydrates 4 g
- Sugar 1 g
- Protein 6 g
- Cholesterol 25 mg

Cinnamon Ginger Cookies

Preparation Time: 10 minutes
Cooking Time: 12 minutes
Serve: 8

Ingredients:

- 1 egg
- 1/2 tsp vanilla
- 1/8 tsp ground cloves
- 1 tsp baking powder
- 3/4 cup erythritol
- 2/4 cup butter, melted
- 1 1/2 cups almond flour
- 1/4 tsp ground nutmeg
- 1/4 tsp ground cinnamon
- 1/2 tsp ground ginger
- Pinch of salt

Directions:

1. In a large bowl, mix together all dry ingredients.
2. In a separate bowl, mix together all wet ingredients.
3. Add dry ingredients to the wet ingredients and mix until dough is formed. Cover and place in the fridge for 30 minutes.
4. Preheat the air fryer to 325 F.
5. Make cookies from dough and place into the air fryer and cook for 12 minutes.
6. Serve and enjoy.

Nutritional Value (Amount per Serving):

- Calories 230
- Fat 22 g
- Carbohydrates 4 g
- Sugar 1 g
- Protein 5 g
- Cholesterol 24 mg

Tasty Peanut Butter Bars

Preparation Time: 10 minutes
Cooking Time: 24 minutes
Serve: 9
Ingredients:

- 2 eggs
- 1 tbsp coconut flour
- 1/2 cup butter, softened
- 1/2 cup peanut butter
- 1/4 cup almond flour
- 1/2 cup swerve

Directions:

1. Spray air fryer baking pan with cooking spray and set aside.
2. In a bowl, beat together butter, eggs, and peanut butter until well combined.
3. Add dry ingredients and mix until a smooth batter is formed.
4. Spread batter evenly in prepared pan and place into the air fryer and cook at 325 F for 24 minutes.
5. Slice and serve.

Nutritional Value (Amount per Serving):

- Calories 215
- Fat 20 g
- Carbohydrates 4 g
- Sugar 2 g
- Protein 6 g
- Cholesterol 26 mg

Conclusion

If you want to start a Low-Fodmap diet, but you don't know how to match the ingredients and what to make food with, Then the Low-Fodmap Air Fryer Cookbook is perfect for you. Follow this cookbook with straightforward instructions, encouraging advice, and You'll save a lot of time and have a healthy meal plan.

Whether you are a low-Fodmap Dieter or just simply a food lover, This book suits you very well. I'm sure you'll like it. Thank you for buying this book. Now let's start your gourmet journey!

www.ingramcontent.com/pod-product-compliance
Lightning Source LLC
Chambersburg PA
CBHW062014090426

42811CB00005B/849